T0196233

RECAPTURING YOUR DIVINE DESTINY

Leaving A Life That's Ordinary - For A Life Extraordinary!

Carole Ann Smith

authorHOUSE®

AuthorHouse™
1663 Liberty Drive
Bloomington, IN 47403
www.authorhouse.com
Phone: 1-800-839-8640

First published by AuthorHouse 9/8/2011

ISBN: 978-1-4634-3493-9 (sc)
ISBN: 978-1-4634-3494-6 (e)

Library of Congress Control Number: 2011911974

Printed in the United States of America

The cost of turning back
on your God-given dream—
is a price too high to pay.

And the price to pay,
to see your dream come to pass—
is priceless.

But thanks be to God,
who gives us the victory through our Lord Jesus Christ.

Therefore, my beloved brethren, be steadfast, immovable,
always abounding in the work of the Lord,
knowing that your labor is not in vain in the Lord.

1 Corinthians 15:57-58

CONTENTS

PRAYER

Oh Lord, we come boldly before Your throne of grace in the name of Jesus Christ.

Help us to dream again. Let our hope rise up in our hearts that we may walk in our calling and reach our divine destiny for our lives—that we may bring You glory.

We ask that You turn our hearts toward You, and light a Holy Ghost fire within us, so that it will cause us to rise up in faith, and walk in our divine plan for our lives.

Renew in us a new passion to serve You, and walk in Your ways, that the world would see Your glory.

Give us a burning desire to do Your will for our lives, that we may bring honor to Your name.

Give us strength to go where You would have us to go, to abound in Your work that You have for us to do.

Give us a new courage to step out in faith, to proclaim Your name to the world, that they may confess you as LORD, and glorify your name.

Give us a new determination to finish the work set before us, that we may reach our destiny.

Help us to rise up in obedience to carry out Your plan for our lives, that the world may see your goodness and praise Your Holy name.

Increase our faith that we may trust You and obey You, and cleanse us from all doubt and unbelief.

Above all LORD, help us in whatever we do, that we would do it as unto You, that we may bring honor to Your name.

Lord we thank You, for hearing and answering our prayers. Lord we thank You, that You are more than able to help us bring our dreams to fulfillment, and we give You glory for it all, in Jesus name.

PREFACE

For we are His workmanship, created in Christ
Jesus for good works, which God prepared
before-hand that we should walk in them.

Ephesians 2:10

I can't think of anything in this world that is greater
than living a dream God puts in your heart. This is a place
of total contentment, peace, and unspeakable joy. It's worth
more than silver or gold or any earthly treasure. Nothing
can compare to walking out the will of God, for your life.

God has a purpose for your life. You didn't just show
up on earth for no reason. You are not a mistake and
your life has a purpose. You are unique and wonderfully
made. You are His **'workmanship'**, or **'work of art'**. No
one else can fill your shoes or do what God has created
you to do. You are irreplaceable, and you were born with a
purpose. You have a divine destiny. You were born to have
a life—extraordinary.

I myself, like the Apostle Paul, a prisoner of the Lord, beseech you to walk worthy of the calling with which you were called. And that you will be fully pleasing to Him, being fruitful in every good work and increasing in the knowledge of God.

You already have the power in you, to bring your dream, or vision to pass. The dream brought to you by the Holy Spirit. No trial, tribulation, or demon in hell, can stop you from reaching your destiny. Once you have grabbed hold of it, with bulldog faith, you are on your way to your destiny. Only 'self' can stop you, if you chose to lay it down and walk away. God who is faithful is with you. His spirit lives in you, to guide and strengthen you, to lead you along your journey.

> For in him dwells all the fullness of the Godhead bodily; and you are complete in Him, who is the head of all principality and power.
> Colossians 2:9-10

It's sad to me, to see so many people with such potential, with gifts and talents, but no ambition, no drive to do anything with what God has blessed them with. They talk about things they would like to do someday, but there is no drive behind them, no fire. They soon wax cold in their dreams, and never experience the joy of walking in there calling. They settle for a life that's ordinary—instead of a life extraordinary.

My greatest desire, as I write these words on these pages, is that it will inspire you to seek God with all your heart. And it will rekindle the God-given dream or vision in your heart that was brought to you by the Holy Spirit. So that you to, can walk worthy of your calling in which you were called.

I, by no means have it all together, but I have lived this in my life, and can testify to what I'm writing. I have lived three of the deepest desires of my heart, and I give the glory to God, who has been faithful, and by my side for each transition of my life to see me through from one dream to the next.

RECAPTURING YOUR DIVINE DESTINY

Everyone has a divine destiny—or some might say a calling. *Recapturing Your Divine Destiny* is a timely message when so many people are out of work. Many have lost their jobs due to the economy, and with the cost of living going through the roof, it's a stressful and trying time for many people. We are living in great tests and tribulations.

But, many times God uses circumstances of our lives to propel us into a new direction. But, the transition can be painful, especially if you have to leave behind something that you love, or in some cases, people you care about. But when God shuts a door, He will open up a window.

It's an awesome time to stop and reflect on your life. Where you are and where you want to go. Maybe you are doing well and you might be feeling a tug at your heart to help others in need. Ask God for guidance and direction and He shall light your path. You might be surprised what ministry lies within you. You may touch one or a thousand lives by your obedience.

"The thief does not come except to steal, and to kill, and to destroy. I have come that they may have life, and that they may have it more abundantly.

John 10:10

It's a great time to look to God, for guidance and answers to your questions. For in Him we live, and have our being. And no matter what comes our way, or what we are facing, He is still in control. He is more than able to carry us through these difficult times, and bring us out on top!

I can't thank of a greater time than now, to pray and seek God, with all your heart, and lean not on your own understanding, but seek Him and He shall direct your path. And reveal your purpose, your calling, so you can reach your divine destiny.

You may be facing a crossroad right now, and not sure which way to go. You may be feeling like God is leading you in a total different direction than what you are on. He may be calling you to a higher purpose—a calling which will lead you to your divine destiny.

That's what this book is about. If God is leading you to do something different; or maybe He's leading you to go where you have never gone before, it will require some work on your part. *It takes faith, courage, sacrifice, perseverance, and tenacity, to fulfill your dream, and reach your divine destiny.* Your divine destiny is a place where at the end of your life on earth, you are exactly at the place—He **ordained you to be.** This maybe your time to move out in faith, and accept His will for your life, to walk in your calling, so you can reach your divine destiny.

Taking the first step is always the hardest. God don't always show us the whole picture, we don't always have all the answers. He doesn't always send us instructions with a blue print showing us how everything will turn out. And this can be scary because we like answers, we like everything in a package; we like to have the results before we take action. But with God we walk by faith and faith has to be tested.

I have lived three of my God-given dreams, and can say each time I had to step out in faith and walk in darkness step by step. It's very difficult to walk where you can't always see what's in front of you. But as I write these words on these pages, I know that He has been faithful in all that I have done. Not all things worked out like I had pictured or imaged, but I know that He was leading me through each transition and He had a purpose for each one.

I like the Apostle Paul, a prisoner of the Lord Jesus Christ, plead to you; to walk worthy of the calling in which you were called. You are unique and wonderfully made in His image. He knew you before the foundation of the world. No life shall be wasted. You were born with a purpose. You were created for a life extraordinary!

I urge you to seek God, for your purpose and calling, so you too can reach your divine destiny. I pray that you will find the courage to step out in faith, to *follow Him* to wherever He may be leading you. Not only will you be glad you did, but the peoples whose lives you touch, through your obedience, will be glad you did too. Obedience is greater than sacrifice.

Maybe you're just starting a new God-given dream, or moving on to your next mission. Or maybe you have a desire in your heart, but just haven't had the courage to step out in faith to get started, God would say to you—

"Fear not, for I'm with you; Be not dismayed,
for I am your God. I will strengthen you, Yes,

I will help you, and I will uphold you with my
righteous right hand.'

Isaiah 41:10

Therefore do not cast away your confidence,
which has great reward. For you have need of
endurance, so that after you have done the will
of God, you may receive the promise;

Hebrews 10:35-36

In order to fulfill your calling to reach your destiny,
you must first surrender to God. You must be willing to lay
down your will, and accept His will for your life. When you
love God with all your heart, you will want to serve Him
with all of your life, with your talents, gifts, time, and in
all that you do.

You must surrender to God, and let the Holy Spirit
guide you in whatever you do? Will you be open to His work
in you, as you go along your journey to your divine destiny?
These questions are a part of fulfilling your divine destiny.

- Are you seeking God, for His plan for your life
  and not your own?
- Will you follow Jesus, wherever He leads you?
- Have you counted the cost that comes with
  your dream?
- Are you committed to your dream, so that you
  won't turn back?
- Will you stand firm in your faith through the
  tests and trials?
- Will you keep pressing toward your dream, no
  matter what comes against you?
- Are you willing to run your race that is set
  before you?

- Will you hold fast to your faith when you are faced with doubt and unbelief?

Remember it's easy to say, "Yes", to these questions when you're on the mountain top, and everything seems bright and everything is going along smooth. But it's another thing to step out in blind faith when the winds of change are blowing, and storms seem to be brewing. And a lot of time that's when God will say, **"Go forward."**

It is by no means an easy or carefree journey, but it's a journey worth traveling. And as you step out in faith, He will be with you every step of the way. We serve a God that is faithful, and is more than able to uphold you with His righteous right hand. He is more than enough, to see you through all that may come against you, and try to stop your dream—your destiny.

> For I, the LORD your God, will hold your right hand, Saying to you, "Fear not, I will help you."
>
> Isaiah 41:13

CHAPTER 1

WILL YOU FOLLOW ME?

To lay down your will,
to follow your Heavenly Fathers will—
is trading a life that's ordinary,
for a life that's extraordinary!

And Jesus walking by the Sea of Galilee, Saw two brothers Simon called Peter, and Andrew his brother, casting a net into the sea; for they were fishermen. Then He said to them, **"Follow Me".** And I will make you fishers of men." They immediately left their nets and **followed Him.** Going on from there, He saw two other brothers, James the son of Zebedee, and John his brother, in the boat with Zebedee their father, mending their nets. He called them. And immediately they left the boat and their father, and **followed Him.**

Matthew 4:18-22

Will you leave all behind, and **follow Jesus**? Will you become fishers of men? Will you leave your will behind, and follow the will of God for your life? Will you let your life bring glory to God?

You're a Christian and you're doing Christian things, you go to church, pay your ties, and participate in church actives—leading a fairly low-key life. Your life requires no real sacrifices, but you're happy. Your life is comfortable. It's ordinary and you're just fine with that. You have some good friends and a nice family, decent job, what more could anyone ask for? Right! It may not be how you dreamed your life would turn out, but you're ok with the way things are. And besides, no one wants to rock the boat when things are going smoothly.

Then suddenly one day you start to feel a tug at your heart—sort of like a stirring of some kind in your spirit. Then the Lord drops a dream, a vision in your spirit, and a new plan for your life. At first you just kind of put it on the back burner, trying not to think about it too much, hoping it will pass, after all, you couldn't possibly do it any way.

But days go by, and it becomes stronger, and then you hear the Lord speak to you. **"Will you follow Me?"** "Will you lay down your will, for the will I have for you?" Your heart knows that God has surely spoken to you. Your spirit knows without a doubt that God is leading you. He's calling you to step out of the boat—out of a life that ordinary and comfortable, and **follow Him** to a life that's extraordinary. *He's calling you to go where you have never gone before, and do something you have never done before.* He's saying. "Will you get out of your comfort zone and **follow Me**? "Will you surrender your will for the will I have for you?" "Will you follow Me and walk out your divine calling—and **follow**

Me to your divine destiny?" A place I pre-ordained for you, before time began, before you called on My name.

You now find yourself are at a crossroad, a place where things change. It a place that represents a cross like the one Jesus was crucified on. It's a difficult place to be. It's were you have to make major decisions that will affect your life; it's a place where your future will change. It's a place where something has to die, before a new life can begin. Sometimes you see warning signs before you arrive at this place, but sometimes you just suddenly find yourself there. Which way will you go, can be a very difficult decision.

At this crossroads things seem different, things don't look familiar, and the crossroad unexpectedly takes on a brand new meaning. It feels different and you feel lead to go a different way. You are being lead to go down a road you have never traveled before, a road that is unfamiliar.

These crossroads can be a place of surrendering your will; for the will of the Father. It's a place where self is crucified; and resurrection of a new life begins. It may be the death of a dream, but the beginning of something greater than the former. Jesus came to a crossroads in His ministry when He was in the garden of Gethsemane, when He cried out, "Not My will but, Yours be done." He gave up His will to follow the will of His Heavenly Father. He chose the cross to fulfill His calling—to reach His divine destiny.

Now you find that the Lord is speaking to you about your life, and you find yourself with a new desire, a new dream in your heart and a new excitement in your Spirit. It seems to consume you, and you find it's all you can think about. You try to keep it quiet and not talk about it. You begin to think if you tell someone, they will probably just laugh, and tell you how silly it sounds. So you keep it to yourself, and then it starts to become like a fire in your spirit, you that you can't put out. It's almost like a consuming fire. It consumes your mind, will and emotions, and your spirit.

Suddenly you now you find your mind and spirit at war with one another. God is asking you to lay aside what is familiar, and comfortable, and move into the unfamiliar, and down a different path than the one you're on. Many questions start to flood your mind. All the "what ifs,' 'maybe this,' 'maybe that's," become your constant companions. Your heart believes, but your mind has doubts. Your spirit says, **"Yes Lord, I will follow you,"** but your mind is saying—no way this is possible.

But as time goes by, the dream becomes like a hunger in your spirit. It has taken over your being, your mind, will, and emotions. It becomes impossible to ignore. Welcome to the point of no return. This is the place where you know that you have to lay down whatever you have to lay down, and leave behind whatever it takes to **follow the Lord,** *to follow your God-given dream, brought to you by the Holy Spirit.*

This is your crossroads, and this is your cross to bear. It's at this point, you must determine whether you will **follow God**, or stay in your safe zone. Will you leave a life that is ordinary—for a life that is extraordinary?

This is a critical time in reaching your destiny. You have to be determined to hold fast no matter what comes your way. This is the time when your adversary will attack. He roams the earth to see whom he may devour. You must be sober, vigilant. You must resist him, be steadfast in your faith without wavering, and trust in God who sent you your dream that He is than able to bring it to pass.

Faith says, "I will stand," with tenacious, unshakable faith, and determination to stand by your word from God, never wavering in faith until you see your dream fulfilled. Nothing else will do; nothing else will satisfy. Nothing else will give you the joy, peace and satisfaction, then walking out the will of God, for your life. It's not an easy journey, but one that's worth it, if you will surrender to God—and just believe.

You can say with the Apostle Paul." I'm now a prisoner of the Lord Jesus and His will for my life. Nothing else matters, nothing else will do." No matter what, I will finish my race. I will reach my destiny. "I will go wherever the Lord calls me to go; I will do whatever He asks me to do."

> But immediately Jesus spoke to them saying, "Be of good cheer! It is I; do not be afraid." And Peter answered Him and said, "Lord if it is You, command me to come to You on the water. So he said, "come," And when Peter had come down out of the boat, he walked on the water to go to Jesus. But when he saw that the wind was boisterous, he was afraid; and beginning to sink he cried out, saying. "Lord, save me!" And immediately Jesus stretched out His hand and caught him, and said to him, "O you of little faith, why did you doubt?"
>
> Matthew. 14:27-31

It's not easy, by any means, to get out of your safe-zone, and walk where you have never walked before, or go where you have never gone before. *It takes great courage, faith and trust to begin your journey*. Peter experienced this when the Lord asked him to get out of his comfort zone in a boisterous storm and come to Him on the water. Peter's spirit was willing, but he looked at the circumstances and didn't continue to trust Jesus. Peter became afraid. But on Peter's behalf, it took a lot of faith and courage to step out on the water, a place where he had never walked before. It also takes even more faith to continue to walk and move forward in your dream when the storms of life are boisterous—when fear and doubt come against you like a mighty rushing wind.

And besides, when Jesus asked Peter to come to Him, and Peter started to sink, Jesus was right there immediately to catch him, to keep him from drowning. In time of trouble, Jesus will show up on the scene and lift you up to solid ground. Jesus will still be there in times of trouble or distress. When the storms come, He is still there.

What a faithful God we serve. What hope and faithfulness we have in Jesus. Even when we fall, He is there, to catch us. Even when we doubt, He is faithful. When we lose our footing, He is right there to pick us up, so we can keep moving forward.

> If we are faithless, He remains faithful; He cannot deny Himself.
>
> 2 Timothy 2:13

It takes a lot of faith and trust to move from where you are, to where God is calling you to go. Most godly dreams are bigger than yourself. If your dream doesn't require you to stretch your faith, and make a change in you, and if it doesn't require you to be totally dependent upon Jesus to bring it to completion, it's probably not a God-given desire, it's probably a fantasy, a dream that will fade with time.

A God-given dream will cause you to have to depend totally on God. And when you depend upon Him to help you see it through, He will change your inner man. He is navigating your spiritual walk, and strengthening your character, and changing you into the image of Jesus; while at the same time, giving you the desires of your heart. He will—

make you complete in every good work to do
His will, working in you what is well pleasing
in His sight, through Jesus Christ, to whom be
glory forever and ever. Amen

Hebrews 13:21

When Jesus calls you out to **follow Him,** it requires obedience on your part, it's a choice. Obedience is the moment when you choose to let God work in you, and through you. It is an outward expression of our love for God. Once Jesus calls you to leave all behind and **follow Him**, you must act on faith. You must have complete trust in Him, that He is all-knowing and knows what's best for you. Faith requires major adjustments in your life. You cannot stay where you are and **follow Him** at the same time. To walk in obedience you must lead a life of surrender to Him, that He may work in you what is well pleasing in His sight. When you are obedient to God, your saying "yes, Lord, I'm available to You, to work Your will in me and through me." To be obedient requires faith and faith without works is dead.

Not only does following the Lord require a surrendered life, but a life that is totally depended upon Him—A heart that says, *"Not my will, but Yours be done."*

"And whoever does not bear his cross, and come
after Me cannot be my disciple.

Luke 14:27

You must be willing to bear the cross that comes with your dream. It may be leaving something you love behind, or giving up something you love. You may have to make great sacrifices. You may feel the sting of rejection by some, or betrayal by others. The cross may become heavy at times.

But be of good courage; Jesus promises He will never leave you or forsake you. He is with you, and He will carry you through the difficult times.

> "And everyone who has left houses or brothers or sisters or father or mother or wife or children or lands, for My name's sake, shall receive a hundredfold, and inherit eternal life." But many who are first will be last, and the last first.
>
> Matthew 19:29-30

If God asks you to give up something, He has a reason. It will be for your good and for His glory. I believe Jesus is saying, "You must be willing to give up any earthly thing that will cause you to stumble, and cause you not to fulfill your calling." You must be willing to lay down whatever He may require of you; you must put Him first, for those who love their lives, will surely loose it, and whoever loses his life for His sake, will preserve it. *Where your treasure is, there will your heart will be also.*

Lots wife is an example of one attached to material things. She could not resist turning around to see what was happening to her home, and as a result she became a pillar of salt. (Gen. 19:26)

I can't think of anything on earth that is worth the loss of eternal life, or your victor's crown. Cars and houses and stuff are nice, and I believe God wants us to have nice things and great finances. God wants to bless His children, so we, in turn can be a blessing to others. But they are not worth losing eternal life for, or forfeiting your divine destiny!

When God gives you your dream, you have to count the cost. Will you forsake all and **follow Him**, to where He wants to take you?

Yet, indeed I also count all things loss for the excellence of the knowledge of Christ Jesus my Lord, for whom I have suffered the loss of all things, and count them as rubbish, that I may gain Christ.

Philippians 3:8

That I may know Him and the power of His resurrection, and the fellowship of His suffering, being conformed to His death,

Philippians 3:10

Paul, counts his loses as rubbish, so he may know Jesus. Paul knew nothing on earth can compare to knowing his Lord Jesus. Paul's sights were on being conformed to God's image and fulfilling his calling. There is not greater accomplishment than this. It's a choice only you can make. Will you **follow Jesus** for a life extraordinary—a life full of blessings and joy unspeakable?

Following the will of God for your life is by no means easy. You will go through trials and tribulations. But the journey is worth it when you know that you are following the will of God for your life. You will find contentment that you can't find outside His will. There is a peace even in the midst of storms and trials that is incredible, when you are in His will and pursuing His purpose for your life. There is a joy unspeakable.

Your journey to your divine destiny is a place where your faith is stretched, and great hope is born, and you grow strong in the Lord.

Your divine destiny
lies at the foot of the cross—
where the blood of Jesus flowed,

with a surrendered heart,
"Not my will Lord, but Yours be done."

And it ends—
When your life on earth is over,
and you are at the exact destination—
that God Almighty ordained before time began!

CHAPTER 2

COUNTING THE COST

All dreams come with sacrifices,
they all come with a price—
but the price you pay to see your dream come to pass,
is never too high to pay!

"For which of you, intending to build a tower,
does not sit down first and count the cost,
whether he has enough to finish it—"Lest,
after he had laid the foundation, and is not
able to finish, all who see it begin to mock him,
"Saying 'this man began to build and was not
able to finish.'

Luke 14:28-30

What is the cost of following your God-given dream?
For each one of us, it is different. But it requires complete
dedication and faithfulness for all who chose to follow God.

It requires a close relationship with the Lord which requires giving up time to spend with Him.

Sacrifices are giving something up for the sake of something else, or the sake of giving something up, for something that may have greater value. All dreams come with sacrifices; they come with a price. Some sacrifices may not seem that big, while others may require you to give up more. Either way, you must be willing to sacrifice whatever God is asking of you. It may be your time, energy, or money; you may have to walk away from relationships, which will hinder you on your journey. You may have to give up earthly possessions, to reach your dream; you may have to leave family behind. Whatever your sacrifice is, you must count the cost. You can't take it lightly. *Deciding to go forward with your dream requires a serious commitment.* You must be committed to God, and committed to your dream to see it through.

Before Jesus went to the cross; He was in anguish, His soul was exceedingly sorrowful. Some sacrifices you face are hard, but needful, to walk in your calling, to reach your divine destiny. **Your divine destiny is a place where, at the end of your life on earth—you are at the exact place where God ordained you to be.**

> And He said, "Abba, Father, all things are possible for You. Take this cup away from Me; nevertheless, not what I will, but what You will."
>
> Mark 14:36

This is an example of a great sacrifice; Jesus laid down His life that we may have life and have it more abundantly. Jesus paid the ultimate sacrifice for mankind. He endured the cross for us, and paid the penalty for our sins, so that we can have eternal life. And in the resurrection He sent us a helper, the Holy Spirit, to transform us into obedient, righteous people.

Remember, it is easier to start a journey when you're excited, and God is speaking. But it takes tenacity, faithfulness, courage, and determination to see it through. You may have to wait weeks, months or even years to see your dream come to pass. You must be able and willing to hold fast, through storms, trials and through the test of time. Your faith will be tested.

> Yet indeed I also count all things loss for the excellence of the knowledge of Christ Jesus my Lord, for whom I have suffered the loss of all things, and count them as rubbish, that I may gain Christ and be found in Him, not having my own righteousness, which is from the law, but that which is through faith in Christ, the righteousness which is from God by faith: That I might know Him, and the power of His resurrection, and the fellowship of His suffering being conformed to His death,
>
> Philippians 3:8-9

The good news is that God would not have given you your dream or desire if He knew you could not finish it. He knows what you are capable of, and most times, more than you. Look at Moses, he argued with God for quite some time, trying to convince God he was not the man for the job. But God chose him for this mission and He knew Moses was more than capable of doing the job. Trying to convince God you are not able to do what He called you to do, is useless.

You already possess the greatest tool you need to bring

your dream to completion. You have the Holy Spirit living in you, to help, guide and strengthen you. All gifts and talents and your calling comes from Him. **Every good gift comes down from the Father of lights, of His own will.**

> John answered and said, "A man can receive nothing unless it has been given to him from heaven,
>
> John 3:27

> But if the Spirit of Him who raised Jesus from the dead dwells in you, He who raised Christ from the dead will also give life to your mortal bodies through His Spirit who dwells in you.
>
> Romans 8:11

And so—
> Trust in the Lord, and do good; dwell in the land, and feed on His faithfulness. Delight yourself also in the Lord, and He shall give you the desires of your heart.
>
> Psalms 37:3

Trials will come, and they will test you. But be encouraged. He who overcame death dwells in you. Hold fast, and He who promised is faithful until your dream's completion. Trust in the Lord, and take pleasure in serving the Lord and He will bring to pass the desires and dreams of your heart. God is faithful.

> But recall the former days in which, after you were illuminated, you endured a great struggle with suffering. Partly while you were made a spectacle both by reproaches and tribulations,

and partly while you became companions of
those who were so treated;

Hebrews 10:32-33

Warning: after you become illuminated or your dream
becomes clear in your spirit, don't be surprised by the
trouble, distress, pain, and hurt you may encounter. This is
when you must hold fast to your faith, and fight the good
fight of faith. You must endure hardship as a good soldier.
You have to keep your vision before your eyes. Stay focused
on where you are going. Stay focused on your God-given
dream and the journey you're on.

> And do not be conformed to this world, but be
> transformed by the renewing of your mind, that
> you may prove what is that good and acceptable
> and perfect will of God.
>
> Romans 12:2

I have learned when God has a plan or a mission for
your life; and you submit to His will, He will bring you to
a place where there is no turning back. And when you have
counted the cost, and you have stepped out of the boat, the
only way to go is **forward**. It may mean you have to work
through doubt, fear, and unbelief as you continue to move
forward, but you must continue and not turn back. One step
at a time, just keep pressing on.

When Moses realized what God was calling him to, he
chose to go forward, and not turn back. He chose to do what
God had called him to do; instead of enjoying the pleasures
of sin, and enjoy a life more comfortable.

> By faith Moses, when he became of age, refused
> to be called the son of Pharaoh's daughter.

15

Choosing rather to suffer affection with the people of God than enjoy the passing pleasures of sin, esteeming the reproach of Christ greater riches than the treasures in Egypt: for he looked to the reward. By faith he forsook Egypt, not fearing the wrath of the king; for he endured as seeing Him who is invisible.

Hebrews 11:24-27

Moses chose to follow his calling, so he could reach his divine destiny. He counted the cost, and moved forward on his journey. He had to leave the comforts of Egypt, the riches of life, the life most men would die for. He chose to follow God even if it meant he had to suffer. He was willing to pay the price and sacrifice earthly riches, to follow Jesus.

When God gives you your dream or vision, you can get prepared for your journey beforehand, by counting the cost and the sacrifices that your dream requires. You can prepare others in your life before hand, if need be.

You should can get excited about your journey ahead, because wherever the Lord is leading you to—has got to be extraordinary!

The cost of turning back
on your God-given dream—
is a price too high to pay?

And the price to pay
to see your dream come to pass—
Is priceless!

CHAPTER 3

TESTS AND TRIALS

With the right attitude—
test and trials
have the ability to produce,
life, strength, hope, and unwavering faith!

In this you greatly rejoice, through now for a
little while, if need be, you have been grieved
by various trials, that the genuineness of your
faith, being much more precious than gold
that perishes, through it is tested by fire, may
be found to praise, honor, and glory at the
revelation of Jesus Christ.

1 Peter 1:6-7

For consider Him who endured such hostility
from sinners against Himself, lest you become
weary and discouraged in your souls.

Hebrews 12:3

Trials and tribulations will come to you on your journey to your destiny. In fact, test and trials will continue after you reach your destiny. But rejoice, because you already possess the strength to overcome them. The strength lives in you as the Holy Spirit. Also, Jesus says, time and time again. "I'm with you; I will strengthen you, and I will never leave you, or forsake you." Jesus encourages us to remember Him when we become weary or discourage in trials, for Jesus endured to the end to fulfill His calling—and reach His destiny.

> Do you not know that you are the temple of God and that the spirit of God dwells in you?
> 1 Corinthians 3:16

Jesus says,
> "These things I have spoken to you, that in Me you may have peace. In the world you will have tribulation; but be of good cheer, I have overcome the world."
> John 16:33

Tests and trials will come, but they are not designed to destroy your faith or bring you discouragement— but to transform and build you up, especially when you step out in faith to fulfill your dream, they show up in many forms. They can show up in some of the most unexpected places. Friends may try to discourage you. Family may not agree with you. You may encounter unexpected circumstances, or your faith maybe tested with fire. Finances may be tested. Obstacles may come against you at times from all directions. You may even begin to doubt your dream, your vision and your destiny.

You may think at times your losing your mind. "What ifs", 'Should haves', and 'Could haves," keep ringing in your ears. But **hold fast**, that which the Lord has spoken to you. Meditate on it day and night, and the day the Lord dropped this dream in your spirit. Stay focused on what is important, and let go of the things that are not. Stay focused on the road ahead. Keep your eyes on the prize, and on Jesus who is faithful and remember; Jesus will keep you in perfect peace as long as you stay focused on Him, and trust Him with all your heart, and your mind.

> You will keep him in perfect peace, Whose mind is stayed on You, because he trusts in You. Trust in the LORD forever, For in YAH, the LORD is everlasting strength.
>
> Isaiah 26:3-4

> And let us not grow weary while doing good, for in due season we shall reap if we do not loose heart.
>
> Galatians 6:9

Remembering what God has done for you in the past; will encourage you to step out in obedience. I believe God takes us step by step from glory to glory. Every trial, test and attack from the enemy has strengthened you along your journey. Look how far you have come. And look what the Lord has done in your life already.

Throughout our lives we are changed and strengthen through each trial we face. What the devil intendeds for evil in our lives, God can and will turn it around, and use it for our good, and His glory. So don't grow weary, you will reap a harvest in due season. Keep focused on the task ahead, and on the One, whom you trust, Jesus Christ.

I can see in my own life each trial I went through, I gained strength, faith, and courage with each one, so when the next trial came that seemed harder than the last one, I was more able to handle it. With each trial being harder than the last, you can look back with confidence and know you are growing in the Lord. This is the only time you should look back at your past; to see how far you have come in faith, strength, courage, and love for the Lord. And give Him glory.

Some trials and tribulations, I have to admit, were very painful and anything but easy to get through. And some of the hardest times, have been when not only was I dealing with one issue; I was hit with a one-two punch—if not more. I felt like I couldn't catch my breath, before I was hit with something else. Like Job, when you're getting hit from all sides, all you can do is hold on to your faith even if it is shaking. Stand firm on the solid foundation which you have begun to build, Jesus being the chief cornerstone. Sometimes it's all you have, when answers can't be found. Just hold on and praise Him in the storm, and He will bring you through.

Shadrach, Meshach, and Abed-Nego were bound and throne in a fiery furnace because they would not bow down and worship the idol at Dura. They affirmed their confidence in God to deliver then from death, but also declared that they would still remain faithful to YAHWEH if He chose not to deliver them from death. And the heat of the furnace was so intense that the men who served as executioners died from sheer exposure to it. And then—

> "Look!" he answered, "I see four men loose, "walking in the midst of the fire; and they are not hurt, and the form of the fourth is like the Son of God."
>
> Daniel 3:25

Glory, glory, and Nebuchadnezzar approach the fiery furnace and called to them and said, *"Shadrach, Meshach, and Abed-Nego, servants of the Most High God, come out from the midst of the fire.* And they walked out. Jesus is there in the midst of the most intense fiery trials that come, and we shall not be burned. Shadrach, Meshach, and Abed-Nego were saved and God got the glory.

I have to admit, during my journey, some of these intense times and fiery trials, my faith was shaking, and I felt like I was going down for the count, and my advisory was winning. I could relate to Job and his excruciating suffering. Job was in such pain he cursed the day he was born. These times are the most trying! There may be times in your journey that the trials become so intense that you feel like you're in a fiery furnace, but He who promised is with you and you shall not be burned. Keep believing and praising the Lord. He will bring you out.

But, to God be the glory, I'm still standing in my faith today, stronger than years past. My love for the Lord has grown deeper and stronger, and my confidence in the Lord to be faithful and do what He has promised, is greater than ever.

During times of testing you have to **hold fast** to your faith and put your trust in the Lord, and lean not on your own understanding. He knows the way you take and when He has tried you, you will come forth as pure gold, refined and able to be used for His glory, so—

> Trust in the LORD with all your heart, And lean not on your own understanding; In all your ways acknowledge Him, and He shall direct your paths.
>
> Proverbs 3:5

No matter what you're going through, God is still in control and nothing takes Him by surprise. He is all-knowing, and nothing can touch your life that doesn't go through Him. We can see this in Jobs life, he lost everything, and yet, he held on to his faith, and trusted in the Lord.

So, if you really know what you are about to undertake is God's will for your life, then **hold on**—regardless of what friends, family, or circumstances have to say. *Follow your spirit, and let it be your guide, today, tomorrow, and forever.*

After you have endured a great struggle with suffering, and you have come through to the other side, you will feel revived and stronger, with more faith in the Lord. And when your vision becomes clear again, hold on to it, and protect it with all your heart. When fiery trials come your way the next time, you will be able to withstand, with more strength, more faith knowing that you will come through more refined than before—for the Masters use.

There is no greater gift that you can give yourself, than running your race and fulfilling you're calling and moving toward your divine destiny. It will not only be a blessing for you, but others will be blessed by you and your obedience. Remember, obedience is greater than sacrifice. It's your duty to fulfill your dream, your calling.

And while you are working out your dream, moving toward your destiny, God is working in you. And this is very good news. He is changing you from the inside, to be more like Him. And as you **move forward,** you will realize in time you have grown in faith, character, hope, courage and determination and most of all, love.

> My brethren, count it all joy when you fall into various trials, knowing that the testing of your faith produces patience. But let patience have

its perfect work, that you may be perfect and
complete, lacking nothing.

James 1:2-4

Fiery trials are test which are purposely designed for
building endurance, in the believer. The word *perfect* means
the 'end' or 'completeness' of a process. Trials are designed
to bring about spiritual maturity and completeness in a
believer. So rejoice if you are going through a trial. God is
working in you what is pleasing to Him. So while you are
working toward your destiny, God is working in you, for
His glory.

being confident of this very thing, that He who
has begun a good work in you will complete it
until the day of Jesus Christ.

Philippians 1:6

You can rest in the assurance that God will complete
the work He has begun in you. You don't have to try to fix
yourself, or your spouse, family, or friends. It's God who will
do the work in you, all you have to do is rest in this promise.
And besides, no real change can come except through the
Holy Spirit. The changes we try to do on our own are usually
just temporary. God will transform you through tests and
trials and by reading and meditating on His word. Godly
character is not made on the mountain top. And, it doesn't
happen overnight. It is a process that takes time.

And not being weak in faith, he did not consider
his own body, already dead (since he was about
a hundred years old) and the deadness of Sarah's
womb. He did not waver at the promise of God

> through unbelief, but was strengthened in faith,
> giving glory to God.
>
> Romans 4:19-20

Abraham held on to his faith so he received his promise because he didn't waver or fall into unbelief. More important, he was strengthened in his faith, and he gave God the glory for it all.

Now let's look at one of the greatest men in the Bible, Job, he was an upright man, blameless and one who feared the Lord and shunned evil.

> Then the LORD said to Satan, "Have you considered My servant Job, that there is none like him on the earth, a blameless and upright man, one who fears God and shuns evil?"
>
> Job 1:8

Job faced one of the greatest trials in the Bible. He lost his family, friends, all his wealth, and even his health in one day—everything gone. Yet he still found it within in himself to praise God through it all. Though He slays me, yet I will still praise Him in the storm. I will praise Him for who He is.

> But He knows the way I take; when He has tested me, I shall come forth as gold.
>
> Job 23:10

Job remained faithful and commitment to God, despite his great trials and lack of understanding. This is the kind of faith that will cause the dream God has given you; to come to pass. This is the kind of faith that will move mountains, and tenacity to reach you destiny. It's this kind of faith that will remove doubt, fear and unbelief in your life.

But you must protect your dream against the forces that try to stop it. How? Stay in close continual relationship with the Lord. Pray without ceasing. Listen for His voice. Renew your mind daily, by reading His word. Fellowship with other believers is a big help. Find someone who believes in your dream or vision and call on them when you need a word of encouragement. This is very important; the road can get rough, and it helps to have someone to lean on from time to time. There is not weakness in this.

> And not only that, but we also glory in tribulations, knowing that tribulation produces perseverance; And perseverance, character; and character hope. Now hope does not disappoint because the love of God has been poured out in our hearts by the Holy Spirit who was given to us.
>
> Romans 5:3-5

Believers glory in trials and tribulations, not because they are fun or easy, most of us would rather do without them. But if handled right they produce godly character, instead of bitterness and frustration. And trials produce perseverance, character, and hope. While weight lifting builds muscle, trials and tribulations build your spiritual man. So no matter what you are facing or going through, remember:

- Perseverance will build endurance, and endurance will build character,
- and character, will give you discernment, and

- hope gives you a confident assurance, for a life extraordinary
- and hope will give you reason to believe in a bright future;
- and love for the Lord will help you carry on, in the face of storms.

When your mind is being bombarded with thoughts of giving up, remember that God will keep you in perfect peace as long as you keep your mind on Him. God has not giving you a spirit of fear, but of power, and of love, and a sound mind.

> For we do not want you to be ignorant, brethren, of our trouble which came to us in Asia: that we were burdened beyond measure, above strengthen, so that we despaired even of life. Yes, we had the sentence of death in ourselves, which we should not trust in ourselves but in God who raises the dead, Who *delivered us* from so great a death, and *does deliver us*; in whom we trust that He will *still deliver us*, you also helping together in prayer for us, that thanks may be given by many persons on our behalf for the gift granted to us through many.
> 2 Corinthians 1:8-11

Wow! Thanks be to God, who always makes us triumph through our Lord Jesus Christ. When we put our trust in Him, He will deliver us in times of trouble. He has delivered us, and is still delivering us, and will deliver us in all trouble and suffering. God showed Paul mercy and he experienced Gods comfort in the midst of great suffering and deliverance from life-threatening experiences.

I know trials and tribulations are not easy, nor are they very joyous at times. In fact; trials can be grievous at times, and they can shake your faith at times. They can be very painful and hard to handle. But they can produce strength, hope, and closeness to God that you can't achieve on the top of the mountain.

Sometimes you may feel as if you are losing your mind, and you're going in the wrong direction. Your perspective may become distorted **for a moment**. It's these times that you have to hold fast to your confession of faith, and bring every thought captive in obedience to Jesus Christ.

If you are to carry out the dreams God has placed in your heart, you must be determined to spend time with the Lord. Being in His presences in the fullness of joy, and the joy of the Lord is our strength.

Trials, if handled right, have the ability to produce life, strength, hope and unwavering faith. Because Abraham did not waver in his faith, he received the promise God had spoken to him. In the natural it was impossible. But with God, all things are possible. He is the Great I Am, creator of heaven and earth and the fullness there of.

> He did not waver at the promise of God through unbelief, but was strengthened in faith, giving glory to God.
>
> Romans 4:20

> I have fought the good fight, I have finished the race, and I have kept the faith. Finally, there is laid up for me the crown of righteousness, which the Lord, the righteous Judge, will give to me on that Day, and not to me only but also to all who have loved His appearing.
>
> 2 Timothy 4:7-8

Use the above passage as a word of encouragement when you need to. I know the journey can be very difficult and tiresome at times. And things we have to face may seem unfair or down right unnecessary, but God who is all-knowing, knows what it will take to fulfill your destiny. He has the whole picture, and we can only see in part. Therefore, we must always put our trust in Him, that He will work everything out for our good.

Job is one of my favorite men in the Bible. This is a man of extraordinary faith. He knew what it was like to suffer. He lost everything, his wealth, children, and his friends didn't help, and even his wife told him to. "Curse God and die". Yet he chose to be faithful and praise God in the midst of a nightmare.

> Then Job arose, and tore his robe, and shaved his head; and he fell to the ground and worshiped. And he said, "Naked I come from my mother's womb, And naked I shall return there. The LORD gave and the LORD has taken away; Blessed be the name of the LORD."
>
> Job 1:20-22

Through all this Job did not sin or did he blame God. This is unshakable faith—a faith that will pull you through any circumstance or attack from the devil. Job went through the grief process; he lost everything, his family, friends, wealth, and even his health. And yet he fell to the ground and worshiped God. Job realized all good and perfect gifts come down from the Father of lights. Job realized he came into this world with nothing, and he was going to leave this world with nothing. Earthly treasures are just temporary pleasures. He knew God is sovereign. And the things we acquire on earth, we will not take with us to heaven. His heart was toward God.

What the devil could not take was Jobs heart and faithfulness to our Lord, which was what the devil, was after to begin with. The devil didn't need his stuff; he wanted his integrity, to insult his character and to destroy his faith. The devil accused Job of only worshiping God because he was blessed of God with earthly possessions. But Job showed his true character, he was a true man after Gods heart, he was a man with integrity and a man who truly worshiped God. Job had a personal relationship with God.

It's God who works all things together for our good. Whether He sent the circumstances or He allowed them to unfold. No matter what God is in control. But Job rose up and did not allow bitterness in his heart to fester. Job did not sin or blame God. He had an attitude of, "No matter what, I'll serve the Lord."

Satan tried to discredit Job to God, but Job was faithful to his faith. He remained true to his belief and trust in the Lord. God is still in control. God was not trying to destroy Jobs faith, but to prove that his faith was real. Tribulations will come, but God is working everything out for those who love Him and have a true heart after Him and worship Him in spirit and in truth.

And at the end, God gave Job double for his trouble, and all things were restored back to Job: his fortune, family, and his future. To God be the glory, who is good all the time—even in the most adverse circumstances.

I can sympathize with Job. I have been through some trials that have taken my breath away. It hurt to breath. I didn't understand why, and I couldn't find the words to pray. I was lost for words. I was at a place of complete brokenness. This was my Gethsemane. My faith was shacking and so was I. Yet, my faith was all I had left, although it seemed very small at the time. This is a place where you have to have complete trust that God is working everything out for your good, and for His glory, no one else can help you, only God can. It's a place that all you can do is surrender to Him, "Not my will Lord, but Yours be done."

I have seen trials and tribulations came so hard at times, that I myself had no clue what I wanted, or needed to happen. But, God who is all-knowing knew. I had to put all my trust in Him, and I knew if He did not help me, then there was no help to be found. I had to have a higher power to pull me through, and back up again. And what little faith I had left, was all I needed to believe that God still had me in the palm of His hand. And one day the Sun would shine again, and I would look back and see the goodness of the Lord.

These times all you can do is cling to your confession of faith, even if it is shaking. At the time you may not have the answers you would like, but you know God does. You may not know what to do, but God does. You have to trust that He is in control and is working everything out, and you have to know that He is faithful. He will come through. It's His promise to you, and He can't go against His character.

> Nevertheless, I tell you the truth. It is to your advantage that I go away; for if I do not go away, the Helper will not come to you; but if I depart, I will send Him to you.
>
> John 16:7

Jesus endured the cross and now we have a helper, the Holy Spirit that helps in times of trouble. In times of tribulation, we have a comforter. We are not left hopeless, or broken. In Him we have a healer.

Hold on to your faith, that has great rewards, and don't

lose heart, in hard times. They will come on your journey to fulfilling your dream, but you can make it through to the other side. You can make it to your Promised Land.

Do not grow weary while doing good, for in due season you will reap, if you don't lose heart. For His grace is sufficient for you, His strength is made perfect in our weakness. And remember that your light affliction is only temporary, or for a short time, and it is working a far more exceeding and eternal weight of glory.

CHAPTER 4

NO TURNING BACK

Once you step out in faith to reach your destiny—
Don't turn back, no matter what.
Keep pressing forward until you see it come to pass.

As you try to move forward on the road ahead of you, discouragement will try to creep in and get you off track. It will come to you through unexpected circumstances, friends trying to talk you out of your dream. Sometimes family members will not approve for many different reasons. You will experience tests and trials like never before. But whatever comes your way, stay focused on what is ahead and keep your eyes on Jesus, and stand firm in your faith. And God will keep you in perfect peace, whose mind is stayed on Him.

You may have to leave behind something or someone that will hold you back from your divine destiny—from your life that is extraordinary. But once you step out in faith to fulfill your dream, just keep walking. You may feel fear of the unknown or doubt may come to your mind, but just keep walking.

> By faith he forsook Egypt, not fearing the wrath of the King; for he endured as seeing Him who is invisible.
>
> Hebrews 11:27

I love this Scripture; Moses did not fear what his enemy could do to him, so he was able to endure his cross. He had his mind fixed on the Lord. And so he was able to bear whatever came against him, and he stayed focused on the journey and the task that was set before him. Moses chose to **go forward**. He chose God's will, rather than following the desires of the flesh. He chose to give up earthly treasures for the sake of his calling—his divine destiny.

> Let us hold fast the confession of our hope without wavering, for He who promised is faithful.
>
> Hebrews 10:23

The Israelites cried out to God for hundreds of years to deliver them from their bondage, but when God sent Moses to deliver them, all they did was murmur and complain. You would think they would never look back, or want to return to their life of bondage to fear, doubt and unbelief. But being in bondage was easier for them to handle, than moving forward into the Promised Land. At least in bondage, they knew what to expect, so it was more comfortable then moving toward the unknown, the unfamiliar.

> Then they said to Moses, "Because there were no graves in Egypt, have you taken us away to

die in the wilderness? Why have you so dealt with us, to bring us up out of Egypt? "Is this not the word that we told you in Egypt, saying, 'Let us alone that we may serve the Egyptians'? For it would have been better for us to serve the Egyptians than that we should die in the wilderness." And Moses said to the people, "Do not be afraid. Stand still, and see the salvation of the LORD, which He will accomplish for you today. For the Egyptians whom you see today you shall see again no more forever. The LORD will fight for you, and you shall **hold your peace**. "The LORD said to Moses, "Why do you cry to Me? Tell the children of Israel to **go forward**.

Exodus 14:11-15

The Israelites were faced with the Red Sea in front of them, and the Egyptian Soldiers with death in their eyes right behind them. It must have looked bad in their eyes for a moment. But glory to God, the Lord had spoken and said, *"I will fight for you," and your enemy whom is right behind you ready to kill you—you will see no more.* And the Lord spoke, **"Go forward"**.

Their enemy was right behind them to destroy them. They had reached their point of no return. If they turned back now they would surely die, so they had to **go forward**. God will bring you to a point that turning back on your dream is not an option, if you do, you will taste death of your dream. For behind you is a place called Egypt, a place of death to all dreams. It's a place of bondage to doubt, fear, and unbelief.

By faith they passed through the Red Sea as by

dry land, whereas the Egyptians, attempting to
do so, were drowned.

Hebrews 11:29

God showed His faithfulness, he showed up in a
powerful way. He parted the Red Sea, so the Israelites could
escape, and He destroyed the enemy at the same time. What
an awesome God we serve!

As you move forward in your dream your enemy may
be right behind you, trying to kill your dream or vision. The
enemy may show up as fear, doubt, unbelief, and even time,
may be your enemy. It may even be something in your past
that's chasing you. But to God be the glory, He is saying,
"Go forward", keep pressing on, and you too, shall see the
salvation of our Lord.

As you move forward, step by step, God will be working
in you. He will be transforming your inner man. He will
strengthen you, and build your faith to new levels, while
polishing your character. You will look back and see that
you are becoming more like Jesus, every step of the way.
He will—

> make you complete in every good work to do
> His will, working in you what is well pleasing
> in His sight, through Jesus Christ, to whom be
> the glory forever and ever. Amen.

Hebrews 13:21

Your dream is as unique as you are. You were created
exclusively for the dream God gave you. There is only one
you and you were designed to be remarkable, just as you
are—and that makes you very special. So the price you pay
to be like someone else is a price too high to pay. Hold on

to who you are, and let God build upon what He created you to be.

The devil, who roams the earth like a roaring lion, seeks to still your dream, kill your vision, and destroy your faith. He will try to still your hope, and stop you from fulfilling your dream. If he can stop you from reaching your potential, and stop you from reaching your purpose; he will have victory over your life.

But God has given you all you need to finish your race; He has given us His spirit as a helper, so one day, you can hear Him say; *"Will done good and faithful servant, great is your reward."* There is no greater accomplishment in this life, than fulfilling your calling, and reaching your divine destiny, a place where God preordained, you to be. And walk where He ordained you to walk.

> Therefore we also, since we are surrounded by so great a cloud of witnesses, let us lay aside every weight, and the sin which so easily ensnares us, and *let us run with endurance the race that is set before us,* looking unto Jesus, the author and finisher of our faith, who for the joy that was set before Him endured the cross, despising the shame, and has sat down at the right hand of the throne of God.
>
> Hebrews 12:1-2

Jesus is the author and the finisher of our faith, and the work He began in us He will complete. So run the race that is set before you, and run with endurance so that you may obtain the promises of God—that you may lay up before you a crown of righteousness.

For consider Him who endured such hostility

from sinners against Himself, lest you become
weary and discouraged in your souls.

Hebrews 12:3

While Jesus was in the garden of Gethsemane, He was in anguish to the point that He was sweating blood. And then He cried out to His Father, *"Not My will, but Yours be done."* He knew the road ahead was going to be a difficult one. He was sinless and now He was faced with bearing all the sins of the world. He despised the shame that sin brings. And if that wasn't bad enough, He was mocked, beaten beyond recognition, spit on, and hung naked on a wooden cross. And His Father had to turn away from Him, He could not look upon His only begotten Son, and I'm sure that was the most painful thing for Jesus, for the first time, He was separated from His Father.

But glory to God, He endured it. *It was His calling, it was His divine destiny.* And now He sits at the right hand of the Father as the King of Kings, and Lord of Lords.

The devil could not stop God's redemption plan, man couldn't stop His divine calling, the cross couldn't hold Him, and death couldn't keep Him in the tomb. Because Jesus was faithful, we are more than able to fulfill our calling, because He sent us a helper, the Holy Spirit, and the anointing that enables us to be strong in the Lord, and help us along our journey so we can walk out our calling. It enables us to bear our cross, to finish our race that is set before us to reach our destiny.

So run your race so you can obtain your heavenly inheritance that is incorruptible, and will never fade away. And rejoice even if for now, you are grieved by various trials. That the genuineness of your faith being much more precious than gold that perishes, through it is tested by fire, may be found to praise, honor, and glory at the revelation of Jesus Christ.

Write your dream or vision down and keep it before you. Press on no matter what, and don't turn back on your divine destiny, which has great rewards. Keep focused on the journey ahead of you. Hold your dream close to your heart, for out of your heart, flows rivers of living water.

Your dream your vision is worth fighting for. It will be worth the journey, it if you don't turn back, no matter what comes against you. When the Israelites were facing the Red Sea, the enemy was right behind them, it must have looked bad from their perspective for a short while—as life sometimes does. But then God showed up on their behalf, and performed a miracle for them. And then God spoke, **"Go forward"**, and I will take care of your enemies. Continue on to your Promise Land—to a life extraordinary.

> Oh, give thanks to the Lord, for He is good,
> To Him who alone does great wonders,
> To Him who by wisdom made the heavens,
> To Him who laid out the earth above the waters,
> To Him who made great lights,
> The sun to rule by day,
> The moon and stars to rule by night,
> To Him who struck Egypt in their firstborn,
> And brought out Israel from among them,
> With a strong hand, and with an outstretched arm,
> To Him who divided the Red Sea in two,
> And made Israel pass through the midst of it,
> But overthrew Pharaoh and his army in the Red Sea,
> To Him who led His people through the wilderness,
> To Him who struck down great kings,
> And slew famous kings,
> Sihon king of the Amorites,

And Og king of Bashan,
And gave their land as a heritage,
A heritage to Israel His servant,
Who remembered us in our lowly state,
And rescued us from our enemies,
Who gives food to all flesh,
Oh, give thanks to the God of heaven
For His mercy *endures* forever.

Psalm 136 (Paraphrased) Footnote: all verses end in, 'For His mercy endures forever'.

CHAPTER 5

IS IT A GOD-GIVEN DREAM; OR JUST A FANTASY?

*A God-given dream is,
like a fire in your spirit—
that you can't put out.*

"Let your light so shine before men, that they may see your good works and glorify your Father in heaven.

Matthew 5:16

Everyone has dreams, even if they never act on them. They all begin with a mental picture or idea, for some it becomes an ambition, a desire that rises up in their heart and spirit. Some learn early on in life what their dreams are for their life, while other it may take years beyond their youth to figure out what it is they desire for their life. But whatever the case may be for you, you must determine between a desire from the Lord or just something in your mind that you might want to accomplish. Is it God-inspired or just a fantasy?

As little children grow up, their minds are full of dreams. They dream of being cowboys, firefighters, some want to be princesses, nurses, and some dream of being movie stars. Whatever their dreams are their little minds race as they play dress up, and play out their character. They have no doubt that they can be whatever their little minds can imagine. When they are hard at playing, they are filled with hope, faith, and sure determination that they will accomplish their goals. They will be what they set out to be.

I can remember growing up and having many dreams of my own. But as time went by, there were three dreams in particular that keep pulling at my heart. They stayed with me into my adult life. The rest of my little dreams just kind of fell by the wayside. Many of them I knew I was not cut out for. I had no real interest or talent in those areas. They couldn't hold my attention.

As you grow up, you learn more about yourself. You learn what your likes and dislikes are—things that you are interest in, and the things that really don't interest you at all. All these things are worked out through time. You learn to discern between a real dream, and just a fantasy.

A fantasy is a dream that wavers. It won't stand the fiery darts from the devil. It won't stand the test of time. You won't have the strength to start them, and you won't have the strength to finish them. A fantasy is just a temporary thought. It passes away with time. It's like a day dream that has no real substance to it. They are not God-inspired.

On the other hand, there are those people who sit back and dream about making things happen. They talk about the plans they would like to accomplish, and dreams they may someday live. But, they never move on them. They sit on a shelf and collect dust, until one day their dreams die, or time runs out. They wax cold in their faith and give up on their dreams. They always put off the smallest tasks; therefore, the big ones never get done. And God says, "If you can't be faithful in the small things, how can I trust you in the bigger things?"

A God-given dream, born of the spirit of the living God, will cause your spirit to leap. It will give you determination to see it through and brought to completion. It's like a fire in your spirit that can't be put out. It will motivate you, and give you the strength to say, "No" to fear. It will cause you to get out of the boat, and go where you have never gone before. To try something through faith, you never tried before. It will cause you to leave the ordinary— for a journey that is extraordinary.

> "His lord said to him, 'Well done, good and faithful servant; you were faithful over a few things, I will make you ruler over many things, Enter into the joy of your Lord.
>
> Matthew 25:21

God-given and God-inspired dreams will cause you to move. If you feed the dream with the word of God, it will cause you to move or you will be miserable. It's like a mandate from Heaven. You can't let it go. Trying to talk yourself out of it will only cause you to become uncomfortable and frustrated. Your God-given dream will take over your being—your mind, your will and emotions, and your Spirit. Just the mention of it, causes your Spirit to leap within you. You can feel it rise up within you when you talk about it.

When God impregnates you with His desires, they need feed, so they can grow and be birthed. It takes work, energy and determination along with faith to bring a God-given dream to completion.

> Commit your way to the Lord; Trust also in
> Him, And He shall bring it to pass.
>
> Psalms 37:5

One of the most important things to remember when you start your journey is that you can't do it on your own; you can't do it in your own strength. If you try to, you will wear yourself out fast. It's the anointing that gives you the strength to carry out your dream. You must depend on God, to work through you to accomplish your dream. And this is where God wants you to be. So in the end, you can say, "to God be the glory, He brought this dream to pass," it's not by might, nor by power, but by the Spirit of the Lord, that will help you to accomplish your God-given dream.

> Do you see that faith was working together with
> his works, and by works faith was made perfect?
> And the Scripture was fulfilled which says,
> Abraham believe God, and it was accounted
> to him for righteousness," And he was called
> the friend of God. You see then that a man is
> justified by works, and not by faith only.
>
> James 2:22-24

So faith without works is dead. If you wait until everything is perfect to step out in faith to move toward your destiny, then you will never move. This is where great faith steps in. There comes a time that you don't need to pray about your dream and your destiny anymore. *All you need to do is, take a step toward your dream, and then another, and soon you will find yourself walking, and then running toward your destiny.* Your destiny is a place where God ordained you to be, at the end of your life.

The Holy Spirit may prompt you to slow down, but a fearful heart and spirit is of the flesh, and it will cause you to stop in your tracks. The flesh doesn't want to step out into the unfamiliar; it likes to know where it's going. It likes to stay in control and know all the details and how the story ends.

But when you step out in faith to start your journey you will find, **this is the place where your faith is stretched, and great hope is born, and you grow strong in the Lord.**

Recapture your divine destiny by weeding out the fantasies and seeking God with all your heart, to stir up in you, His will for your life. And let the Holy Spirit guide you on a journey of a life-time. It's a journey worth traveling.

CHAPTER 6

PRESSING TOWARD YOUR GOAL

Keep pressing toward your goal, your dream, and your vision.
Be steadfast without wavering in faith—
and it will lead you to a life extraordinary!

Not that I have already attained, or am already perfected; but I press on, that I may lay hold of that for which Christ Jesus, has also laid hold of me. Brethren, I do not count myself to have apprehended; but one thing I do, forgetting those things which are behind and reaching **forward** to those things which are ahead. I press toward the goal for the prize of the upward call of God in Christ Jesus.

Philippians 3:12-14

You may have a new dream in your heart, or one you laid down years ago. Maybe you have made a new commitment to God, and He has placed in your heart, a new desire, a new dream or a new vision. Whatever the case may be, you are ready to step out in faith to make it happen. God has given you a release to move on your dream, or vision. You may be feeling really excited about the journey you are about to take. And you should be; you found the courage to step out of the ordinary and press toward the extraordinary. You have decided to walk out your calling to a divine destiny and this is something to be excited about, and it's something to rejoice about. Making the decision to walk where you have never walk or go where you have never gone before, is the first step to your divine destiny.

The excitement begins to bubble up in you and you can't wait to get started. Then suddenly out of the clear blue, your mind begins to race back in time. Your mind begins to remind you of your past. All the things that you did that failed. All the mistakes you made in your life. Some things you may not be proud of, and your mind stars to wonder if you have what it takes. *"What if's," "Should haves", and "Could haves,"* start to become all you think about. You begin to wonder if God really did speak to you. This is just a trick of the enemy to get you off your path.

Welcome to the enemy called, *"your past."* Everyone has one. Everyone has to overcome something that they have done, or something someone has done to them. But be encouraged, nothing up till now can disqualify you from your destiny, only if *you* choose to lay your dream down and walk away from it. We have second chances with God, and some of us have had to have more than that. We have a God who is just, and ready to forgive us, and cleans us from all unrighteousness, fear, doubt, and even unbelief. He has promised us, He would complete the work He began in us. He would never leave us or forsake us.

When the storms come against us on our journey we will stumble. All of us have stumbled at times in our journey, as long as we are absent from the Lord, we are in the flesh. But the important thing to remember is; you can get back up and dust yourself off and keep on going. Keep on pressing toward your destiny. Jesus is already there to pick you up.

The past can rear its ugly head at any time in your journey, but it seems to come at the worst time. (Hint: it's the trick from the enemy) Just when you feel your making progress, and things are going along pretty smooth, it comes knocking at the door of your mind. You let your guard down, and entertain just one memory, one negative thought, and before you know it, it takes over your mind and you begin to doubt. Fear creeps in, and your courage seems to be sinking, just like Peter when he got out of the boat to walk on the water to Jesus. Peter was a man that was a professional fisherman, grew up on the seas, but he suddenly became afraid of a Ferris storm, and he began to sink. But Jesus was there to pick him up. Doubt, fear, and unbelief are ways the enemy tries to stop you in your tracks. But, glory to God, Jesus will still be there. He will pick you up and set your feet back on solid ground.

When your mind is bombarded with negative thoughts, just take a deep breath, and redirect you thinking. Your mind really is the battlefield. This is the place where it is easy to give up. But Jesus says, *"He will keep you in perfect peace whose mind is stayed on Him."* Doubt and fear comes from the mind (from the enemy). If you think about it, the devil does not want you to fulfill your destiny, why would he, he is an enemy of God. He has come to still, kill and destroy your dream, your destiny. He doesn't want you to stand before the Lord, so Jesus can say, "Well done good and faithful servant, great is your reward; enter into the joy of the Lord." But hold on, the devil is a lie. The battle of the mind can be won, through renewing your mind and a close relationship with the Lord. You should use these times to run to God.

> And do not be conformed to this world, but be transformed by the renewing of your mind, that you may prove what is that good and acceptable and perfect will of God.
>
> Romans 12:2

This is why it's so important to stay in a close relationship with the Lord, renewing your mind daily, praying, and relying on your support team—even if it is just one person who believes in your dream. Talk to them, lean on them if you grow weary, when things get tough and they will at times, let them pray with you. I believe that drawing close to God is personal, for each one of us it different. For myself, it's always been through praise and worship, yet, there are times that I can't get enough of the word. You have to find what works for you.

This enemy is designed to bring discouragement. He tries to make you feel you're not worthy to have such a dream, or you don't have what it takes to finish your race. After all, who do you think you are? How could you think God could use a person like you? He will try to use your past against you. And when he does, you just remind him of his future. His time on earth will soon be over. And besides with God, old things pass away, all things become new.

> Therefore, if anyone is in Christ, he is a new creation; old things have passed away; behold all things have become new.
>
> 2 Corinthians 5:17

Let's look at Paul; he was going around persecuting the

Lord, murdering the disciples of the Lord. I'm sure Paul was astonished that Jesus would choose him. But Jesus called him a chosen vessel of His. So Paul went from persecuting Jesus, to preaching the gospel. And all who heard Paul speak were amazed. And Paul, increased in strength and confounded the Jews, and proved to the Jews in Damascus Jesus is the Christ. Paul had quit the past, yet, Jesus still chose him—and what a tremendous work He done in Paul.

So the good news is, God chose you, before the foundation of the world. He knows about your past, he even knows your future. He is fully aware of what you are capable of. And He is able to up hold you with His righteous right hand. God doesn't make mistakes. Unlike us in human form, God is perfect in all His ways.

The past is what it is. You can't change it, no matter how much you might like too. Therefore; the only time you should look at the past, is to see, how far you have come, so you can testify to the good works of the Lord. He is your Alpha and Omega, all things begin with Him, and all things end with Him.

If you dwell on the past, you will not move forward. It will hold you hostage, and your faith will not grow. You will forfeit your divine destiny.

> But Jesus said to him, "No one, having put his hand to the plow, and looking back, is fit for the kingdom of God."
>
> Luke 9:62

You have to choose to walk away from the past, start living in the present, so you can move on to a bright and remarkable future. If you don't believe God can accomplish in you; what He has designed you to be, then you have believed an evil report. This is why it took the Israelites forty years, to enter the Promised Land, they believed an evil report, they believed there were giants in the land and they became afraid. It was their mind-set that caused them to be afraid, and doubt what God had spoken to them.

God gave Abraham, a great man of faith, a promise, and a dream. And Abraham made many mistakes along the way to his promise, yet he keeps his heart open to God, and he received his promise. And now Abraham is called the father of many nations and a friend of God.

Some of the greatest men and women I know have come from a past. They were serving the world and not God. We have all have sinned and fallen short of the glory of God. We were all born into sin and have a sin nature. But by grace we have redemption through our Lord, Christ Jesus.

And now to hear them preach or speak they are amazing. You would think that they have always walked with the Lord. But at some point, God called them, *"Will you surrender your will, for the will I have for you."* They arrived at a crossroads, and they had to make a decision. Once you accept Jesus as your Lord and savior then your future changes. This should give all of us hope. It's amazing how God calls the most unlikely to serve Him in mighty ways.

> Jesus said to His disciples, "If anyone desires to come after Me, let him deny himself, and take up his cross and follow Me.
>
> Matthew 16:24

The Bible is filled with great and mighty men, and women of God, who missed up along their journey. And some felt unworthy to serve Him. But they were able to move past the past; and go on to do mighty things for God, for our edification, and encouragement. In turn we should encourage others along their journey. Therefore we should comfort each other and build up one another.

> Let nothing be done through selfish ambition or conceit, but in lowliness of mind let each esteem others better than himself. Let each of you look out not only for his own interests, but also for the interests, of others.
>
> Philippians 2:3-4

God, who has shown mankind grace and mercy through His Son Jesus Christ, can show you mercy and forgiveness to move you forward to a bright future, your destiny—to a life extraordinary.

> So I will restore to you the years that the swarming locust has eaten, the crawling locust, the consuming locust, My great army which I sent among you. You shall eat and in plenty and be satisfied, And praise the name of the Lord your God, Who has dealt wondrously with you; And My people shall never be put to shame.
>
> Joel 2:25-26

I myself can testify that through my career as a Professional Driver, that God hammered in my one life changing principle—He is faithful, and will do what He promised in His word. He will be with you through the good times and the hard times. *He is the great I Am*. It makes no difference what people say, but rather, what God says. *And when He gives you a word, you can take it to the bank and deposit it.*

Be encouraged to keep pressing *forward*, through the storms that may come and the trials that may test your faith. I can say God is faithful He will not lead you wrong no matter what the circumstances say or people around you say. Stay surrendered to His leading, and let Him lead you to your divine destiny. To a life that is extraordinary.

Your journey to your destiny
is where great hope is born,
your faith is stretched,
and you grow strong in the Lord.

It will be worth the effort if you will continue on,
No matter what comes your way.
It's a journey worth traveling.

CHAPTER 7

WALKING IN FORGIVENESS

Forgiving others heals your wounds,
forgiving yourself—
releases you,
so you can **move forward**, *on your journey.*

"And whenever you stand praying, if you have anything against anyone, forgive him, that your Father in heaven may also forgive your trespasses. But if you do not forgive, neither will your Father in heaven forgive your trespasses."
Mark 11:25-26

Forgiveness is to excuse for a fault or offense, to give up anger or resentment against. If you let unforgiveness linger in your heart it's like a poison that affects your whole being. It will affect your whole life. It will affect your decisions, your health, even your relationships with others and with God.

If you harbor unforgivness in your heart, it will keep you captive and hold you back on your journey. You will be trapped in that moment of time. *And it becomes hard to walk forward, when you have the weight of unforgivness pulling you back in time.*

I have seen this in many people who were hurt or done wrong and they just can't seem to move on. They spend most of their time meditating on what others have done to them or said to them. That's all they seem to talk about. *They become a prisoner to the hurt by not letting it go.* And this affects everything in their lives. It becomes a poison that affects their future decisions and affects future relationships with others as well as their relationship with God. They get stay stuck in the past, so they are blinded, and therefore, they can't see what is in front of them. They can't see the rainbows for the rain.

Unforgivness will also affect your relationship with God. **It becomes a wall between you and God, you can't get past it— and God can't get through it.** And the wall becomes higher and higher and you soon become isolated, as though you are behind prison walls.

I know some hurts, that come our way, can be very painful and hard to forgive at the moment they happen. But you have to forgive by faith, and soon the feelings will catch up with your emotions. You will wake up one day and realize that the offence doesn't hurt anymore, and all the bad feelings have disappeared. This doesn't usually happen overnight. You just have to keep saying, "Lord, I forgive them, they know not what they do, In Jesus name."

I urge you, don't get stuck in the past because someone has hurt or wronged you. Your relationship with God is more important than anything that can come against you in this life on earth. And your future and your health are so much more important, than anything the other person has done to you.

Jesus who endured a horrifying death by being crucified on a cross cried out; *"Father forgive them, for they do not know what they do."* Jesus is our example. I'm not sure we can really wrap our minds around or understand the pain they put our Savior through, or understand what He must have been feeling. But we do know that it was a terrible and horrific death. Yet, through it He was able to forgive his accusers.

Walking in forgiveness is huge, for the Christian walk, it's not a choice, and at the same token you have to forgive yourself. In my early years as a Christian, this was one of my biggest issues I had to deal with. I found it easier to forgive others, than myself. I had set my own standards so high that I couldn't reach them. Even now twenty-six years later, I still at times find it hard not to be so hard on myself. I really have to work at not letting the enemy fill my mind with mistakes I have made. So, I have had to learn to let go or I wouldn't have been able to accomplish what I have. I have to keep reminding myself who I am in Jesus. Thanks be to God, I have made progress in this area, I have not arrived, but I'm not where I used to be.

> casting down arguments and every high thing that exalts itself against the knowledge of God, bringing every thought into captivity to the obedience of Christ.
>
> 2 Corinthians 10:5

I think one of my biggest hang-ups for me, not being able to forgive myself was, and I had the wrong idea of what God expected from me. I wanted to try to fix myself first, but I soon realized that, I in my strength couldn't fix myself.

I had the wrong idea of what a Christian was. I was working too hard, to try to fix myself without success. It was sort of like being on a treadmill, walking hard and fast, but not going anywhere. It is God who does the work in us, so that He can work through us. The cross says, "I'm redeemed by the blood of the Lamb. I'm worthy because of what Jesus did on the cross.

God, through His power, grace and mercy and the blood that Jesus shed on the cross can change us on the inside, and make us whiter than snow. Only through God, can real change take place. And it doesn't happen overnight. I wish I could say it did. But it is a process that takes time. I have learned through hard times that we serve an awesome God. He is able to make the crocked paths straight; He is able to fix a broken clay pot. He can fix the brokenness in us—that life sometimes hands us. He knows the way we take and when He has tried us, we shall come forth as pure gold. Refined and ready for the Masters use. There is no condemnation in Christ Jesus.

Many times your accusers are more damaged than you are.

> being confident of this very thing, that He who has begun a good work in you will complete it until the day of Jesus Christ;
>
> Philippians 1:6

You can rest in this promise that God will complete the work in you that He started. He knows how much heat it will take to refine you into a vessel of honor, into the image of His Son Jesus. So when you look in the mirror, you will see Jesus looking back at you.

Therefore, my beloved, be steadfast in your journey. Press toward the goal that is set before you, not wavering off the path, but be steadfast, and you can accomplish your goal, fulfill your dream, and reach your divine destiny. Which will lead to a life extraordinary? You will walk with greater faith, strength and love for the things of God, which is a sign of maturity.

> And this commandment we have from Him; that he who loves God must love his brother also.
>
> 1 John 4:21

> Beloved, if God so loved us, we also ought to love one another.
>
> 1 John 4:11

Keep pressing **forward**, now may the God of peace Himself sanctify you completely; and may your whole spirit, soul, and body be preserved blameless at the coming of our Lord Jesus Christ.

He who calls you is faithful. And Jesus says, "My grace is sufficient for you, for My strength is made perfect in weakness."

> And He said to me, "My grace is sufficient for you, for My strength is made perfect in weakness," Therefore most gladly I will rather boast in my infirmities, that the power of Christ may rest upon me. Therefore I take pleasure in infirmities, in reproaches, in needs, in persecutions, in distresses, for Christ sake. For when I am weak, then I am strong.
>
> 2 Corinthians 12:9-10

God's strength is made perfect, complete, and mature in

our weakness. For when I'm weak, then I am strong through Christ's power.

Now may God of hope fill you with all joy and peace in believing that you may abound in hope by the Holy Spirit. And you will keep on keeping on your journey to reach your divine destiny—to a life extraordinary.

> not lagging in diligence, fervent in spirit, serving the Lord; rejoicing in hope, patient in tribulation, continuing steadfastly in prayer; distributing to the needs of the saints, given to hospitality. Bless those persecute you; bless and do not curse. Rejoice with those who rejoice, and weep with those who weep. Be of the same mind toward one another. Do not set your mind on high things, but associate with the humble. Do not be wise in your own opinion. Repay no one evil for evil. Have regard for good things in the sight of all men. If it is possible, as much as depends on you, live peaceably with all men.
>
> Romans 12:11-18

CHAPTER 8

RUNNING YOUR RACE

God has been preparing you
for such a time as this —
to live your dream and reach your destiny!

Do you know that those who run in a race all run, but one receives the prize? Run in such a way that you may obtain it, And everyone who competes for the prize is temperate in all things, now they do it to obtain a perishable crown, but we for an imperishable crown. Therefore I run thus; not with uncertainty, thus I fight; not as one who beats the air.

1Corinthians 9:24-26

An athlete is one who is trained for physical feats, or one who competes in competition. To be a great athlete, you have to train. It takes time to build up strength and endurance. It takes discipline and faithfulness to reach your goals. Such training can be challenging and sometimes difficult at times. It's during this time you must poses, tenacity, desire, even faith to believe you will hit the mark, and you will finish the race and reach your goal.

In your life as a Christian, God has been preparing you for this time, this moment, when He would reveal His plan for your life. He has been personally training you step by step, building in your character and endurance. He has been strengthening you along your personal journey. He is your personal trainer. He knows how much pressure to apply; He knows how much heat it will take to mold you for His purposes in your life. Before you called upon His name, He knew yours. He knows what you are capable of. He knows your strength and weakness. He knows how to personally train you, so you can compete in the race set before you. God has had you in training your entire life. No trial or test will go to waste. He works all things together for your good and His glory.

> for it is God who works in you both to will and to do for His good pleasure.
>
> Philippians 2:13

Like Jesus, you have to be committed to the race, no matter how difficult it may be. Jesus clearly did not enjoy the cross. In fact, He despised the shame. But He endured the cross, because He had His sight on fulfilling His purpose, His divine calling, to reach His divine destiny. And He submitted to the Father's will.

> Then He said to them, "My soul is exceedingly sorrowful, even to death. Stay here and watch with Me." He went a little farther and fell on His face, and prayed, saying, "Oh My Father,

> if it is possible, let this cup pass from Me;
> nevertheless, not as I will but as You will."
>
> Matthew 26:38-39

Jesus was in agony, to the point that he was extremely grief-stricken, but He endured the cross. He finished the race. He was committed, faithful and now He sits at the right hand of the Father.

If you are willing to pay the price, with a humble spirit, submit your will to your heavenly Father, and fight the good fight of faith, then you too, can finish the race that is set before you. You can endure your cross to fulfill your dream; you can have a life extraordinary, and walk with God, with more faith, more courage, greater character and faithfulness.

> And let us not grow weary while doing well,
> for in due season we shall reap if we do not lose
> heart. Therefore, as we have opportunity, let us
> do good to all, especially to those who are of the
> household of faith.
>
> Galatians 6:9-10

Be determined to hold on to your faith, even in trials and tribulations when it seems to be shaking. Make the decision you will finish the race that is set before you. Stay in the race, and do not lose sight of the finish line. And God can say to you, "Well done good and faithful servant. Great is your reward."

> We are hard-pressed on every side, yet not
> crushed; we are perplexed, but not in despair;
> Persecuted, but not forsaken; struck down, but
> not destroyed-always carrying about in the body

the dying of the Lord Jesus, that the life of Jesus
also may be manifested in our body.
2 Corinthians 4:8-10

No matter what comes, hold fast to your God-given
dream. Trials may come from all sides; and we may even
be confused at times. We may be persecuted and knocked
off our feet from time to time, but we are not—crushed,
forsaken or destroyed. No matter what comes, hold fast to
your dream, you are more than a conqueror in Christ Jesus.
You can finish your race, and see your dream fulfilled. His
Spirit is manifested in our body. Let it be your strength, let
it be your guide, so you can move from a life that's ordinary
to a life extraordinary!

> Seeing then that we have a great High Priest
> who has passed through the heavens, Jesus the
> Son of God, let us hold fast our confession.
> For we do not have a High Priest who cannot
> sympathize with our weakness, but was in all
> points tempted as we are, yet without sin. *Let
> us therefore come boldly to the throne of grace
> that we may obtain mercy and find grace to help
> in time of need.*
Hebrews 4:14-16

In our weakness we can come freely before the throne
of grace, we can speak with confidence, that God will show
us mercy and grace and lift us up. God is not so high, that
He can't sympathize with our weakness.

Your journey may seem long and hard at times, it can
even cause you to become weary at times, but be encouraged,
God is able to supply you with strength and energy, even to
the most weary. He will give you the anointing to walk out

your calling. Even athletics that train hard and long, and are in top condition, will grow tired and weary at times. But God's strength is available for all who wait in patience for His purposes to be carried out.

> Even the youths shall faint and be weary. And the young men shall utterly fall. But those who wait on the LORD shall renew their strength; They shall mount up with wings like eagles, They shall run and not be weary; they shall walk and not faint.
>
> Isaiah 40:30-31

Our God never sleeps nor does He grow weary. He gives power to the weak. He will give you the strength to finish your race. His strength is available for all who will call upon His name. His ways and thoughts are so far above ours, sometimes we just have to wait for just a moment, and He will renew our strength. And you will soar like an eagle, with strength and grace. God resists the proud, but gives grace to the humble.

> You are of God, little children, and have overcome them, because He who is in you is greater than he who is in the world. They are of the world. Therefore they speak as of the world, and the world hears them. We are of God. He who knows God hears us; he who is not of God does not hear us; By this we know the spirit of truth and the spirit of error.
>
> 1 John 4:4-6

Therefore be encouraged to leave behind a life that is ordinary—for a life that is extraordinary. Run your race with certainty that is set before you, with confidence and assurance that God is more than able to bring you through to the Promised Land, your divine destiny. A place that is flowing with milk and honey—A land that flourishes with heavenly blessings.

I plead to you, to walk worthy of the calling with which you were called. Submit yourself under the mighty hand of God, that He may exalt you in due time. Stand firm in your confession of faith that will cause you to finish your race. Look toward Jesus the author and the finisher of your faith. He is the Alpha and Omega, the begging and the end.

When Jesus died on the cross, He gave us the Holy Spirit as a helper in our journey to fulfill our calling. So you can run your race with confidence, hope, and faith that He who promised is faithful and will see you through to your destiny.

You were born for such a time as this, to live your dream. And reach your destiny that God pre-ordained from the beginning of time. **And at the end of your life you can say, "I have done the will of God for my life."**

CHAPTER 9

BEING FAITHFUL

*Without faith you can't
reach your divine destiny—
it's the one thing you can't live without.*

Now faith is the substance of things hoped for,
the evidence of things not seen.

Hebrews 11:1

Without faith it is impossible to please God. Faith says, "I trust You Lord, I believe in You, and I'm fully confident in You." Without faith you can't receive salvation, or believe God is who He says He is, or receive his promises. Nor can you walk out your Christian life without it. It's the one thing you have to **hold fast** too. **It's the one thing you can't live without.**

Faith lays the foundation of all things hoped for. Your faith must be solid, with unshakable confidence in God. It must be built upon the assurance that He will be faithful to

His promises—He will be faithful to you. He is all-knowing and all-powerful. And He cares for you.

> By faith Abraham obeyed when he was called to go out to the place which he would receive as an inheritance. And he went out, not knowing where he was going. By faith he dwelt in the land of promise as in a foreign country, dwelling in tents with Isaac and Jacob, the heirs with him of the same promise; for he waited for the city which has foundations, whose builder and maker is God.
>
> Hebrews 11:8-10

Unshakable faith says, "Yes, Lord, I'll go wherever you lead me, or do whatever You require of me." Even though Abraham had no idea where he was going, or where the road was leading him, he stepped out in faith to be obedient. To set out on a journey, without knowing where you're going, takes a great leap of faith and complete trust in God. And Abraham was faithful, and he received the promise.

I experienced this in my own life. God had spoken to me and said, "Move to another state," a place where I knew no one. It took a lot of faith, and courage, but I was sure God had spoken. It was a place that I had never been before. But I went, and God was with me. Friends thought I had lost my mind. And, I guess I did, because it wasn't my mind leading me, it was my spirit. And many watched me, ready to see me fall.

What I soon discovered when I arrived at my destination, was God had everything worked out. My job, where I was going to live unfolded like a flower in spring. I have to admit that even I was amazed at how things worked out. At the time, all I knew was He said *"Go, and I'm with you."* But

He, who sits on the throne, had already gone before me, and arranged my steps and gave me favor. And then, nine months later, He spoke to me again and said, "Go live your next dream, and do not be afraid, I'm with you."

When God is in it, He will bring you through till the end. And God did, He proved His faithfulness, and when my work there was done, He moved me on to my next assignment—my next God-given dream. This was not only a great blessing to me, but many others as well. It was for my good, but for God's glory. This was a time when God was stretching my faith and was teaching me to be totally depended upon Him. He used this time to refine and build me up to new levels in Him.

I bring this point up because there will be those who doubt that God is in your dream, or directing your steps. They may proclaim that you have lost your mind. Why would God request such a feat? But, God's ways are really not our ways. Many said, "God doesn't speak to them." I'm still surprised how many people don't believe that God speaks to us today. But God doesn't change; He is the same, yesterday, today, and forever. But there will be some along your path that won't see God's hand in your journey, but don't let this bring doubt to your heart and mind. Not everyone will accept you, or see what God is doing or trying to accomplish in your life. *All that matters is that you be obedient to His will, and follow His leading.* It's the humble that He guides and teaches His ways. And, we were bought at a price, so we should not become slaves to men, but serve God in spirit and in truth. *So be led by the Spirit, today, tomorrow, and forever, at let it be your guide.*

> For we walk by faith not by sight.
> 2 Corinthians 5:7

God may ask you to walk were you have never walked before, or go where you have never gone before. You will have to step out in total faith and dependence on Him. You must believe that He can and will bring you to the place that He is leading you to. This is the place where you must be faithful in your faith. And come to a place that no matter what the circumstances are or what others are saying, you will *follow Him*. It may not even make since to your mind, but that's ok. He will lead you step by step. God's is in control. He is the good Shepherd; and He knows His sheep, and His sheep know Him. And the Scriptures say, "Whoever believes on Him will not be put to shame."

> You were bought with a price; do not become slaves of men. Brethren, let each one remain with God in that state in which he was called
> 1 Corinthians 7:23-24

The things of God to the unbeliever are foolish. And even some believers say God doesn't speak. But God is the same yesterday, today, and forever. He doesn't change. Jesus says, *"He who has ears to hear, let him here!* You have to be tuned into the Holy Spirit to fulfill your divine destiny.

> Beware lest anyone cheat you through philosophy and empty deceit, according to the tradition of men, according to the basic principles of the world, and not according to Christ.
> Colossians 2:8

This Scripture is huge in following your dream. God moves in ways that the unbeliever can't understand. His ways are foolish to them, that do not believe, and His ways are so far above ours, we must let the Spirit lead us. I know if I have the choice to listen to friends or God, no matter how it may look to some, I'd rather listen to what God says. I know friends are important to our lives, they can be sounding boards, and they can be there for us when we miss the mark, and they can give us support along our journey. And godly friends are very precious; they are worth more than gold or silver. It is wise to seek godly council. But sometimes, God may ask you to do something that no one else will understand. Others can't always see the whole picture, or what God is trying to do in your life. It's at this point that you have to make a decision, to follow man or follow the Spirit of the living God.

> "By this My Father is glorified, that you bear
> much fruit; so you will be my disciples.
>
> John 15:8

Noah for example, had a word from God; he must have looked foolish to many, building an ark in the desert. But Noah walked with God, and Noah found grace in the eyes of the Lord. Noah did that which God commanded of him. So despite what the circumstances said, or the people around him, he chose to obey God.

And the rains came, and it rained until the whole earth was flooded, and all perished except for Noah and his family and all the animals the he gathered upon the earth. Noah didn't look so foolish any more. But when he started his project, his journey I'm sure everyone laughed and teased him. But, to God be the glory. He was faithful to do what He had promised and Noah was obedient and was saved.

There are so many examples of men and women in the Bible that were faithful to God and what He instructed them to do. And many things probably did look foolish through the eyes of the world. I find it interesting that God does things in ways that only He can take the credit for, and be praised for. Mankind that thinks there so smart, with the technology and hi-tech information, can't even compare to the knowledge and awesome ways of our Lord. He is truly an awesome God and greatly to be praised in all that He does, and in the way He carries out His will, and purposes for our lives. He is simply amazing.

> By faith the walls of Jericho fell down after they were encircled for seven days.
>
> Hebrews 11:30

Joshua told the people "do not speak a word until I tell you to." And on the seventh day they marched around the city seven times, and Joshua gave them the order to "shout", and the walls fell flat. Not exactly how many of us would take a city and everything in it. But God had spoken, and Joshua was obedient. He was faithful to the Lord, he trusted God. **For God's ways are not our ways; and His thoughts are not our thoughts.** I find most of the time; God does things in strange ways. Prayers are answered, but not always in ways we think, or imagined.

Fight the good fight of faith, so you may obtain the promises of God. Do not cast away your confidence, which has great rewards. And may God find you faithful in all you do.

Faithfulness is such a great character trait to have in all you do, in your job, family, and your relationship with God. *Unless you are faithful to the journey ahead of you—you won't make it to your destiny.* In all that we do for the Lord requires faith in Him, and faithfulness to carry it out.

Obstacles will come against you to try to get you off your path, this is for sure. But by holding fast to your faith, and being faithful to the task in front of you, you can accomplish your dreams— you can live a life that is extraordinary. Just make up your mind that *no matter what*, you will continue in faith, which is your foundation, built upon the chief cornerstone, which is Jesus Christ.

It's easy to give up on what God is calling you to do if you're not faithful. Just every day issues will come along to get you distracted, to get you off track. You have to be faithful in prayer, fasting, and fellowship with God, if you are going to finish the race set before you. Faithfulness takes great discipline.

God needs dependable people to carry out his plan; we are His hands and feet right now upon this earth. In turn we must depend on Him to finish our calling, and reach or divine destiny. He is a rewarder of those who diligently seek Him. He is with us in fear and trembling, and those who put their trust in Him, shall not be put to shame.

> But thanks be to God, who gives us the victory through our Lord Jesus Christ. Therefore, my beloved brethren, be steadfast, immovable, *always abounding in the work of the Lord*, knowing that your labor is not in vain in the Lord.
>
> 1 Corinthians 15:57-58

Abraham is a prime example of being faithful in his faith. He followed where God led, and believed the promises God made. He was faithful even when God asked Him to sacrifice his son, whom he loved so much, and waited for, for such a long time. He followed where God was leading him, and prepared to sacrifice his son because God asked him too. I'm sure Abraham must have been heartbroken when God made such a great request. But in spite of what he was feelings, he chose to obey God.

- Faith say's, I trust God. No matter what
- Faith say's, I'm totally depending upon Jesus and seek His guidance in daily decisions.
- Faith grows with time, through trials and tribulations, and by experiencing God's faithfulness.
- Faith gives the Holy Spirit control over your life.

I encourage you to stay focused on your journey, on the course God has put you on to fulfill your divine calling, so you can reach your divine destiny. You were born for such a time as this. You were created for a purpose beyond just living and breathing. You are unique and wonderfully made. You were born for a reason. I encourage you to seek God and **follow Him.**

You may have to go where you have never gone before, or do something that you have never done before. But He is with you. He will never leave you or forsake you. You may start your journey scared, but as you **move forward**, each step gets easier, each step builds character, faith, hope, and love for God.

You might be surprised at what you will, and can accomplish as long as you stand firm in your faith, and steady in your faithfulness. And your eyes fixed on Jesus.

If you will reach for the stars—
You may just touch Heaven!
And Heaven just might come down to you!

CHAPTER 10

MOSES:
FROM RULER, TO SLAVE, TO DELIVER

The death of one dream is not the end—
But a chance to fulfill
a dream greater, than the former!

Moses was a prince of Egypt. He was an heir to the throne of Egypt—an heir to wealth, power, earthly treasures, and a life with a beautiful women.

Then a day came when he realized who he really was. Up until then, He had been living a lie his entire life, not by his choice, but by the choices others made for him. No matter what you do, or where you go, you can't run from who God created you to be. Moses was living a life as a prince with the hope that one day he would become ruler over Egypt—the next he became a slave. Moses plans for his life where not the one's God had for him.

One day a ruler the next wondering in the desert with the heat from the sun beating down on him. Thirsty and weary, **he moved forward**, by a force unknown to him—*with a calling on his life and a destiny, that was yet to be revealed to him.* He keeps pressing on.

This was Moses broken road, one paved with the death of one dream to lead its traveler to God; to a higher calling, for a divine destiny. He continued to travel a path through the wilderness to a destiny he did not know where it was leading him. Yet he was compelled to keep moving onward.

He chose to lay down his dream of being a ruler, to follow the God of Abraham, Isaac, and Jacob—**the great I Am.** Not fearing the wrath of the king. He chose to suffer affliction with the people of God, rather than enjoying the passing pleasures of sin. He refused to be called the son of Pharaoh's daughter. He held the reproach of Christ in higher esteem than the treasure in Egypt; he endured as seeing Him who was invisible. He looked to his reward, and his heavenly calling.

Letting go of a dream God has given you is by no means easy. It can in fact be very painful; it can cause you to question a lot of things. It can cause your faith to shake. But I can say that if God asks you to lay your dream down, whether it is a God-given dream or a dream born of your own flesh, and leave it behind, then He has something far more glorious than the former dream.

When God first spoke to me about letting my first dream go, I had to obey through tears, and a lack of understanding at the time. But a few days later I got a word from God, *"In seven days your life will never be the same."* And in seven days, my life changed in a way I could not have imaged, or the way I imaged it would be.

At the time I was in an abusive marriage and I felt like I would never be able to get out. Through my eyes there was no way out, it was my Egypt. I had been praying for years for God to deliver me out of this circumstance, but I couldn't see anyway this could happen. But God heard my cries, and through unexpected circumstances, He propelled me out. There was no time to thank about leaving, or how I would survive. I was out, and there was no turning back. God had delivered me from bondage; He delivered me, from my Egypt—my life of bondage to fear; death of spirit, and a life of abuse. But in order for Him to deliver me, I had to let go of my God-given dream, so He could lead me out of Egypt. Let go of what lies behind and look forward to the greater things ahead.

Not only was this the beginning of the healing process for me, from all the things which I had suffered for nearly twelve years. God was preparing me for my third dream. A dream that was more awesome than the former. It would be the dream that changed me the most and drew me closer to Him, more than anything else had in the past. It was a dream that required more faith, courage, strength, and determination and complete trust in Him.

It's hard to let go of a dream that you birthed and watched grow and mature. Your dream becomes such a big part of your being. It's like your child; you nurtured it, and watched it grow. You put your heart and soul into it. It took all your faith to start it, and it took all your faith to let it go.

Moses thought he would soon be ruler over Egypt, but God had other plans for his life, and God would soon reveal His awesome plan to him. But before He could, Moses had to choose to follow God. He had to let one dream die, so God could fulfill another one, greater than the former. Greater than anything Moses could have imagined—a destiny with heavenly treasures that can't be destroyed, a destiny with *a higher calling, and purpose.* Moses's broken road soon became a bridge to a life greater than he could have ever dream of or imaged.

One of the hardest things in our walk with the Lord is letting go of people, things, and dreams, especially if you have your heart, soul and time invested in it. But I have found that, when God asks you to lie something down, and let it go, He has a reason. He has the whole picture; He sees where you are, and where He wants to take you. We may not always have the answers we want at the time, but God does, and this is where unshakable faith and trust come in.

My first God-given dreams were to be an artist and writer. After I graduated from art school many years ago, I couldn't find a job in my area for a Graphic Artist. So I got a computer and started a home business. As demand grew, I bought one piece of equipment and then another, until I had my own business. Then, God dropped a vision and a dream in my spirit for a Christian Magazine. So I started writing and using my printing business to print it. I had my printing business for about five years, and I wrote for three years. Even though my circumstances were bad at the time, I felt as though I was walking on cloud nine. And for that, I would not have change that time growing in the Lord for nothing.

Then God spoke to me and said, "Lay it all down, and follow me." "Shut down the business and leave it behind."

Now I loved what I was doing, and all that I could think of was, "Why?" *Why would God bring me this far and then ask me to sacrifice my dream, that He gave me?* My mind was a blur and my heartbroken. I was so broken I couldn't see where the road was leading too. My heart was shattered, and I felt as if I was going in the wrong direction in life.

And if losing your dream is not bad enough, people and so called friends can be very cruel and can say mean things. Friends and family are not always sympathetic, or understanding. They want answers, but many times we don't always have the answers at the time. But we trust Him, who does.

Unknown to me at the time God was preparing me so He could deliverer me out of my Egypt. He was being faithful. He was in fact, answering my prayers, just not like I had thought He would. My little mind had it all figured out in a different way.

> Then He said, "Take now your son, your only son Isaac, whom you love, and go to the land of Moriah, and offer him there as a burnt offering on one of the mountains of which I shall tell you."
>
> Genesis 22:2

Abraham loved his son, he waited a long time for his promise from God, and now God, was asking him to sacrifice him. *How could God make such a demand, and more than that, why would He?*

It was God who made the promise to Abraham; he would be a father of many nations. And now God was asking him to sacrifice his seed, his only son—whom he loved so much.

But Abraham obeyed. The next morning he gathered his stuff and his son and set out for the mountain that God would lead him too. But, when Abraham arrived God spoke again to Abraham, *"Lay not your hand on your son, I know you fear God, because you have not withheld him from Me."* *"I will provide the sacrifice.*

God had merely been testing Abraham. I'm sure Abraham must have been heartbroken, when God spoke this request to him. He waited a long time for his son and to lose him now, in this way would have been heart breaking.

I know when God asked me to lay down my first and

second God-given dream, I thought I had failed God and was being punished. But God is good all the time, and His ways are not our ways. At the time, what I thought was a failure, was really God setting me up for my third dream, which was bigger than the former, which took greater faith, courage, and trust in Him. It was a dream that at the time I had no idea of how it would bring me closer to God, and transform me into the person who God called me to be. But it allowed me to overcome a lot—and let go, of much more.

> "For My thoughts are not your thoughts, nor are your ways My ways." says the Lord. "For as the heavens are higher than the earth, So are My ways higher than your ways. And My thoughts than your thoughts.
>
> Isaiah 55:8-9

During a time of transition, you have to hold on to your faith, even if it is shaking. Transition is a hard place to be. It's a place where everything seems upside down or things are out of place. It's uncomfortable, because the road becomes broken. But hold on tight to the truth that you have. During this time it also helps to remember how God had worked in your life in the past; how He moved you from situations in the past; how He closed doors and opened windows. How He was faithful in other circumstances.

> And we know that all things work together for good to those who love God, to those who are called according to *His* purpose.
>
> Romans 8:28

God can't be put in a box; His ways are so much higher

than ours. He is all- knowing and knows what's best for us, and how to accomplish things in our lives, for our good and His glory.

Not all God-given dreams are to last a life-time. They may last for just a season. He may move you on to bigger and greater things as you grow in strength, courage, faith, hope and love. As you grow and bear more fruit of the spirit God, may move you to accomplish even greater things, for His glory and for His Kingdom. But in order for Him to move you, you must be willing to lay aside the former things which you have labored and cared about. Although it may be hard at the time, it will be worth the next journey He is leading you on. Be steadfast, immovable, always abounding in the work of the Lord, knowing that your labor is not in vain in the Lord.

So whether you are just starting a dream or moving on to your next assignment, God would say,

> "Fear not, for I'm with you, be not dismayed, for I am your God. I will strengthen you, yes, I will help you, and I will uphold you with my righteous right hand.
> Isaiah 41:10

> Therefore do not cast away your confidence, which has great rewards For you have need of endurance, so that after you have done the will of God, you may receive the promise;
> Hebrews 10:35-36

So the death of one dream does not mean it's your end, or that God is finished with you. It may be that He is moving you to something bigger, something greater than the former.

Carole Ann Smith

Moses went from ruler of Egypt, to a slave in the desert, to a deliverer of God's people. He went from believing one thing about himself, to becoming the man God created him to be.

CHAPTER 11

BEYOND THE BROKEN ROAD: IS A NEW GOD-GIVEN DREAM, A NEW JOURNEY!

When all you have left is your faith—
then hold on to it tight,
do not throw away your confidence,
which has great rewards!

We are hard-pressed on every side, yet not crushed; we are perplexed, but not in despair; Persecuted, but not forsaken; struck down, but not destroyed.

2 Corinthians 4:8-9

You will face trials and tribulations on our journey to your destiny, but we are not at a loss, or left hopeless, or damaged by the circumstances that we may encounter along the way. Even if you don't have all the answers, you can trust God

Carole Ann Smith

in whatever may come your way. He will light your path as you move forward in your journey.

It was twelve years later after letting go of my first and second God-given dreams, God spoke to me again about my next assignment, a dream I never really talked about, kind of a secret dream. After all, there was no way I could accomplish such a task. It was a dream I had always had in my heart, but never thought I would ever be able to achieve. After all, there is no way I could do it.

Then on a warm sunny day, I was traveling on vacation. I stopped at a lookout point located over a river in Tennessee, and God spoke, "Go and get your CDL's (Commercial Driver's License) and travel the country and do not be afraid, I am with you." To my mind this was crazy. Although it had always been a dream, I never thought I would really do it.

Besides, I had a twelve year career going. And I was self-supportive, what if I failed? I didn't have anything to fall back on. "What ifs," kept going through my mind. But every time I began to doubt what the Lord had spoken, the vision, the desire became stronger and stronger. The vision was before me day and night. I saw in the spirit me accomplishing this great and awesome venture. It became so clear, and real that no one could talk me out of it, or tell me I couldn't accomplish this.

> For God has not given us a spirit of fear, but of power and of love and of a sound mind.
> 2 Timothy 1:7

People around me thought I was going through some kind of mid-life crises. They let me know how dangerous it was, how mean people are in the world, etc. But I knew in my spirit, God had spoken. I knew He was leading me. And my thoughts were, "If God is leading me, and He was the one who ordained this, then He was more than capable of keeping me safe." I didn't doubt that it was dangerous, but I knew God was with me. And I will have to admit I was scared, and trembling. But I knew I had to move forward in spite what I was feeling. After all, the spirit is willing, but the flesh is weak.

I was unsure what was ahead of me, or what was around the corner, but I knew, God had spoken. Therefore I had to walk in faith, with total dependence on God. For I knew if He was not in this then, I would not make it. But it wasn't like I had never made a mistake before.

Faith without works is dead.
And without faith it is impossible to please God.

In the following months I caught the vision. I saw in the spirit realm I was driving this huge truck. It grew stronger and stronger each day. Every time I would see a big truck going down the highway my heart would leap. In three months I was register at a CDL School, and in three weeks I received my CDL's. I was now qualified to drive an eighteen-wheeler. I was on my way to fulfilling my God-given dream—and a journey of a life-time.

> Jesus said to him, **"If you can believe, all things are possible to him who believes."** Immediately the father of the child cried out and said with tears, "Lord I believe; help my unbelief!"
>
> Mark 9:23-24

Then the tests and trials began—

As a new driver (student just coming out of school)

you have to go out with a trainer, which is assigned by the company that you chose to work for. This process should last about four weeks, and then you are assigned your own truck.

The purpose of going out with a trainer is to learn and gain skill in handling an eighteen-wheeler. Your success can depend on whether or not you get a good trainer. One who cares if you get the training that you need to further your career. Unfortunately, I got a trainer who did not care whether or not I got the training I needed to move up to a first-seat driver, their only concern was making extra money for me being on their truck.

As a result I suffered greatly, and did not get the training I needed or deserved. In fact, my trainer said, "I would never make it as a driver," and was always putting me down and yelling at me. It was, to say the least; the most trying and frustrating time for me. I could not understand why I had to suffer so greatly. I knew God had ordained this mission. This shouldn't be this hard. At the time I couldn't understand what God was trying to accomplish or what was really going on. So, my mind started to doubt the vision that was so strong before me just a few months earlier.

But deep within my spirit I knew I had to keep going. And soon my spirit rose up to a new level and I was strengthened, so I was able **to keep moving forward.**

As time went by, it became clear to me that this mission I was on wasn't about a job, it was about what God was trying to accomplish in me, so that He could work through me. My faith in what I believed, keep me steady and strong, it was the one thing no one could take from me. So I keep pressing on with the vision before me, and because it was so strong and unshakable, I was able to withstand the darts of the enemy. Now it was not easy and it took all I had in me, to hold onto my faith. It was through tears and much trembling, that I held fast to my confession, and chose to believe God, rather than man. I had to pray without ceasing, and depend totally on God, to see me through to the end. But God had already spoken, "Do not be afraid, I'm with you." He is with us in weakness, fear and much trembling. He is with us each step of the way.

> But recall the former days in which, after you were illuminated, you endured a great struggle with suffering;
>
> Hebrews 10:32

I have to admit that I was almost ready to give up, and then suddenly, the Lord sent me an angel—not an apparition with wings, but a person who changed the course I was on. He was able to calm every fear, every doubt that tried to take over my mind, and my spirit was renewed. And in fourteen days, I got my own truck and never looked back. I took the wheel, and God as my Co-pilot, I taught myself how to drive. And God was with me and He proved His faithfulness to me in a mighty ways.

God used this experience to lift me up and let me prove to myself that in Him, nothing is impossible. And, this experience taught me so much about the strength that lies within me. And the tenacity and endurance that lies within me, to keep going when things get hard, to trust Him, when the road becomes unclear, or the circumstances don't seem to line up with the word I received from Him. *And the most important—my love for the Lord has grown stronger than ever and my faith and trust has risen to new levels.*

I soon became one of the top drivers of the division I was on. So not only did I make it, but I became great at what I was doing. So I pressed forward and done it as unto the Lord, and I was able to sow seed, from the east, to the west, form the north, to the south. And God deserves the credit, because He proved not only His faithfulness, but his divine protection and favor. For when I was weak, He made me strong—through His Spirit.

This adventure will go down as one of my greatest accomplishments. Not because I can drive a semi across country, this joy was not about my job, but what God did in me. It may not seem like a very godly job, but I saw it as a way of drawing closer to God and a time for Him heal me from so much hurt that I had suffered. At the same time I was able to see His wonderful creation, which brought incredible peace and appreciation for God creation. The United States is so beautiful, and I'm so glad I was able to see it. It brought me great joy.

So dreams that seem impossible to reach—are possible for those who dare to believe. For those who put their trust in the Lord. *I went from a job and a life that was ordinary—to a job and a life that was extraordinary.*

So I can testify to the fact that with God—your dreams can and do come true. He is more than able to uphold you with His righteous right hand. And if your God-given dream comes to an end, then hold on, because the next one will be greater than the former. For your latter days will be greater than your former. God is faithful who promised that He would never leave you or forsake you. He is still there in the midst of your storms. Like Peter, He will reach down and pull you back up and set your feet on solid ground.

The devil will send circumstances to try to get you off track, to try to get you to let go of your dream. But hold on; believe in the One who is more than able to keep you from falling. Keep trusting in Jesus who endured the cross, despising the shame, and now is seated at the right hand of God, our Father.

The road that once, seemed broken and fragmented

at the time has become a bridge, to a new life, down a new road—that has been greater than anything that I could have dreamed of or even imagined.

Hold fast to your confession—
This has great rewards.
And set up heavenly treasures
where neither moth and rust destroys,
Run your race with endurance
that after you have done the will of God
you may receive the promise.
For God is a rewarder of those, who diligently seek Him
And He will lead you from a life that's ordinary—
to a life extraordinary!

CHAPTER 12

MY DREAM, MY JOB, BUT GOD'S GLORY!

Your job, whatever it maybe, has the potential
for growing your faith, and make you stronger and
bring glory to the Lord!

While we do not look at the things which are
seen, but at the things which are not seen. For
the things which are seen are temporary, but the
things which are not seen are eternal.

2 Corinthians 4:18

I have been through some horrific things in my life and to
see where I am today in my faith, character and love for
God, amazes even me. It's only because I held on to my
faith, even if it was only the size of a mustard seed. It was
enough.

As I look back on my driving career which doesn't seem
very glamorous or even a godly desire has turned out to be

the most incredible life changing and faith builder in my life, thus far.

When I started this adventure, I was not sure myself, why God would give me such a strong desire to do this. But when I look further back on my life, I can remember when I was five years old, my family and I were traveling on the West Virginia Turnpike, and I saw these big rigs up close and I told my dad, "I'm going to drive one of those trucks one day." Of course he blew it off, as most dads would. But God— on the other hand, had a plan and a purpose for this dream, this desire. He knew all about my life and what I would go through. God already saw my future. I believe God planted that seed in my spirit then, long before I could possibly understand the need of it in my life. This dream was for an appointed time. ***It was my dream, It was my job, but it was all for His glory.***

As I started my journey toward my driving career, God, the great I Am, was with me through the storms, through the fire. He stayed faithful to what He promised me on the day He told me to, "Go and be not afraid, I'm with you." So I went and there were times I became afraid and trembling, and had become weak, but He was with me. And He brought strength back to me to help me keep going forward.

It was the most incredible journey. He showed up especially in the most difficult times and always sent someone across my path, in times of trouble to lend a helping hand. And He will do the same for you.

> Now may the God of hope fill you with all joy
> and peace in believing, that you may abound in
> hope by the power of the Holy Spirit.
> Romans 15:13

Each one of my God-given dreams has made me stronger, as a person, and as a Christian. I gained more confidence, faith, strength and learned to totally depend on God. I learned more than ever how faithful God really is, even in times when I didn't understand what He was doing.

But as a driver of a big rig, this was the job that enforced in me the greatness of His mercy and grace, and brought me to a full understanding, of His unwavering faithfulness. It enforced in me character and strength. It brought me to a place of peace with myself. It had been a long time since I could say, that I was proud of what I was able to accomplish with His help. But more than that, I learned how to totally depend upon Him, and only Him. I learned I could trust Him. I have always believed Him, but I don't think I really ever fully trusted Him. I know if it wasn't for Him, I would not have made it.

Driving a big rig requires great discipline, courage, commitment, and great sacrifices. It's a job that not just anyone can do. Because it's a job that can be grueling and very demanding at times; it requires great endurance. It may not seem like a very godly job, yet it's a job that is so important—America really does roll on eighteen-wheels. All the things most people take advantage of, like food, clothing, gas, furniture, all the things that make your life comfortable, is transported by truck. Professional Drivers do deserve great respect, on the road and off the road.

Your job may not be about the work, but the lives you can touch through it. It maybe your job, but it may be all for the glory of God.

Each one of us has the potential for ministering hope and love toward others each day. Opportunities come our way more often than we think to minister to others. All we have to do is be open to the Holy Spirit to lead us. There are people in our daily lives that need a word of encouragement, someone to talk to, maybe a financial need. There maybe someone along your path, that just needs someone to pray with them. And a lot of time, people just want to be heard.

You may feel like your job is not a godly job, but if you will allow God to work through you're your job it can transform you, and bring glory to His name. You have the potential at your place of employment, whether you're a homemaker, or a vice president of a big company, to spread love and hope, and a word of encouragement along your way. You have the ability to let your light shine before all men, that they may see your good deeds, and glorify God and praise His name.

> For our light affliction, which is but for a moment, is working for us a far more exceeding and eternal weight of glory? While we do not look at the things which are seen, but the things which are not seen. For the things which are seen are temporary, but the things which are not seen are eternal.
>
> 2 Corinthians 4:17-18

God has a plan and a purpose for all who will believe. When you step out to follow God to fulfill your dream, many things will come against you. But know that you can accomplish what God gives you to do. Most of all let God work through you, as you walk out your calling to your divine destiny.

I have been blessed to have lived all three of my dreams. But the thing that astounds me the most about my journey is, the change that has taken place in me, in my heart and my spirit. As I look back on my life twenty years ago, and see where He has brought me from, is amazing to me. And I know God will do the same for you.

I know what it's like to be broken and
I know how to get back up.

I know what it is like to be weary from the journey and
I know what it takes to keep going.

I know what it is like to be discouraged and disappointed,
But I know that God knows what's best for me.

I know what it is like to be knocked down,
And I know how to reach up and take Jesus by the hand.

I know what it is like to try to walk in the dark,
And I know what it's like to find the light again.

I know what it is like to face the devil and
I know I am more than a conqueror in Christ Jesus.

I know what it is like to lose everything and
I know what it is like to rebound and find hope again in
Jesus.

I have known great sadness and affliction and
And I have learned to sing praises to the Lord again.

I know what it's like to pull away from God,
And I know how to draw near to Him again.

I know what it's like to be persecuted for my faith,
But I know my Redeemer lives.

I know what it's like to suffer greatly,
But I know in Jesus I have love, joy and peace.

I know what it is like to lose my way and
I know what it's like to find my way again.

I have gone from artist and writer to driving a semi across the country. I have walked away from each of my dreams with more character, faith, hope and a greater love for Jesus. With a since, I have helped a few along my way. I'm not saying this to boast, because it is not I, that do these good deeds, but Christ that lives in me. I have just allowed Him to work through me.

He knows the way we take and when He has tried us, we shall come forth as pure gold. You will be molded for the Masters use, giving Him the glory that is due His name. We are His workmanship, unique and wonderfully made.

Whatever you eat or drink, or whatever you do, do all to the glory of God, and—

> "Let your light so shine before men, that they may see your good works and glorify your Father in heaven.
>
> Matthew 5:16

> Then Jesus spoke to them again, saying, "I am the light of the world. He who follows Me shall not walk in darkness, but have the light of life."
>
> John 8:12

CHAPTER 13

A HEART SURRENDERED TO GOD— IS A HEART OF WORSHIP

To reach your greatest potential,
your God-given dream—
you must live a life of surrender to
our Lord and King!

Then I will give them one heart, and I will put a
new spirit within them, and take the stony heart
out of their flesh, and give them a heart of flesh.
That they may walk in my statutes and keep my
judgments and do them; and they shall be my
people, and I will be their God,

Ezekiel 11:19-20

A heart surrendered to God, is a heart of worship!

Will you worship Me?
Will you give me your heart?

<u>Will you give me your everything?</u>

Your journey toward your destiny is where you will find that your faith is stretched, and great hope is born, and you grow strong in the Lord! And transform you into the likeness of Jesus.

When you love God with all your heart, you will want to serve Him with your life. With your talents, time, and in whatever you do. Will you surrender to the Holy Spirit and let it be your guide today, tomorrow and forever? Will you be open to His work in you, as you go along your journey to your divine destiny? A place where when your time on earth is through, you will be at the exact place where God ordained you to be.

Will you surrender your all to Jesus? Will you accept His will for your life? Will you trust God enough to put your hopes and dreams totally in His hands? Will you turn your life over to Him and surrender everything Him?

All these questions are a part of fulfilling your divine destiny.

- Will you follow Jesus, where He is leading you; will you surrender to His will?
- Are you counting the cost that comes with your dream?
- Are you willing not to turn back on your dream once you step out of the boat?
- Will you hold fast when the tests and trials that comes your way?
- Will you keep pressing toward your goal to fulfill your calling, no matter what?

- Will you run with tenacity the race that is set before you?
- Will you be faithful in your faith when trials come?

These seem to be really simple questions that most people would say, "Yes" too. But it's one thing to say, "Yes" when everything looks bright and everything is going well in your life. It's another thing to follow God when you are not sure where the road is leading, when you don't have all the answers to your questions.

But be encouraged to follow your dreams and reach for your divine destiny. I have learned through my journey, that in all my dreams I never got the whole picture of how it was going to turn out. Not all things have worked out like I thought. But to God be the glory, He used all the test and trials, even the good stuff in my life for my good, and His glory. I had to just step out in faith, in obedience and leave the results up to God. My life is in His hands, and He is more than able, to keep us from falling. Trusting in Him, who is more than we need, is a form of worship.

> Those who trust in the LORD are like Mount Zion, Which cannot be moved, but abides forever As the mountains surround Jerusalem, so the LORD surrounds His people from this time forth and forever.
>
> Psalm 125:1-2

> Was not Abraham our father justified by works when he offered Isaac his son on the alter? Do you see that faith was working together with his works, and by work faith was made perfect? And the Scripture was fulfilled which says,

"Abraham believed God, and it was accounted
to him righteousness." And he was called the
friend of God.

                        James 2:21-23

May the Lord be with you, in all that you do.
You were created with a purpose
You are unique and wonderfully made
for such a time as this.

My you find the courage to step out in faith,
and move from a life that is ordinary—
to a life that is extraordinary!
In Jesus name.

*To recapture your divine destiny—
just surrender to His will,
and let Him lead you to your divine destiny.
For a life that is extraordinary!!*

*And when your life comes to an end upon this earth,
like Jesus—
you can be at the exact place, where God ordained you to be.
and
you can say, "I have done the will of God for my life."*